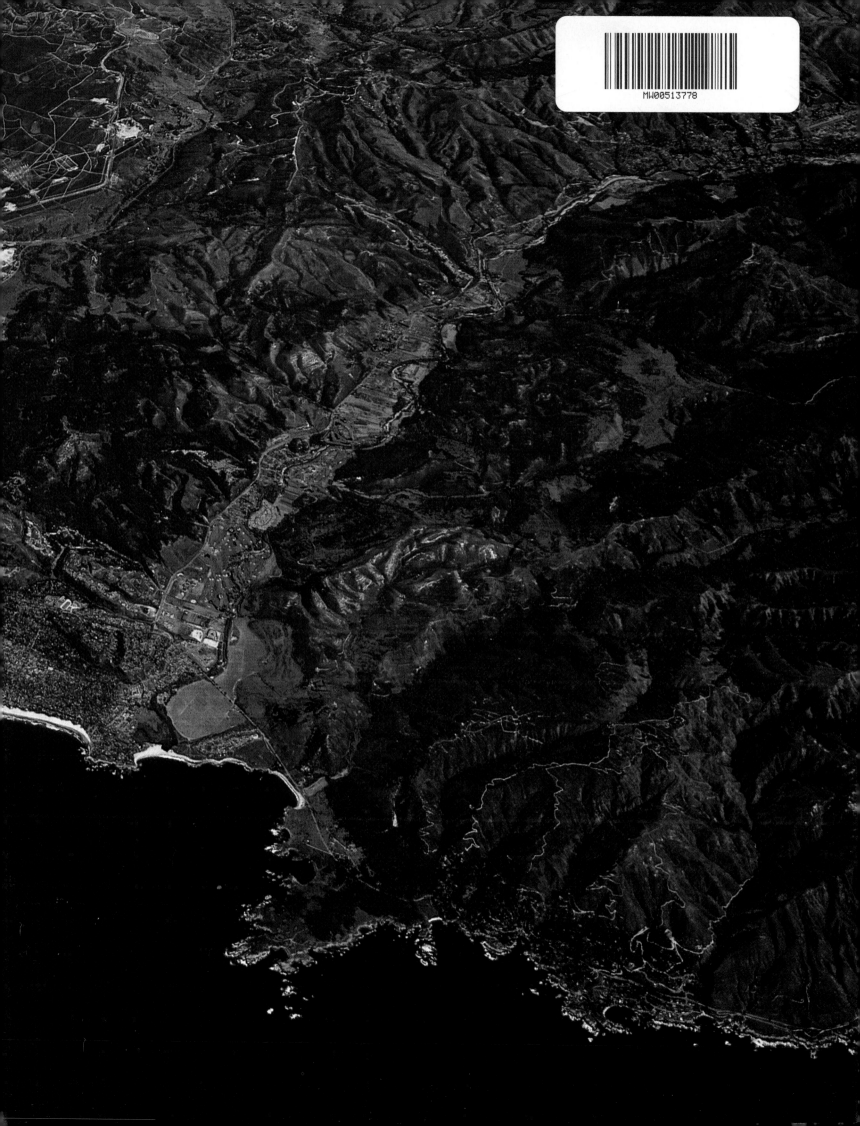

A PARADISE CALLED
PEBBLE BEACH

▼

BY RAY A. MARCH
AND THE
EDITORS OF GOLF DIGEST BOOKS

Published by:

 Golf Digest/Tennis, Inc.
A New York Times Company
5520 Park Avenue, Box 395
Trumbull, CT 06611-0395

Distributed by:

POCKET BOOKS, a division of Simon & Schuster Inc.
1230 Avenue of the Americas
New York, NY 10020

ISBN: 0-671-77722-X

Library of Congress Cataloging-in-Publication Number: 92-71487

First Golf Digest/Tennis, Inc. Hardcover Printing April 1992

10 9 8 7 6 5 4 3 2 1

GOLF DIGEST/TENNIS, INC. and logo are trademarks of
Golf Digest/Tennis, Inc., A New York Times Company.

Printed in the U.S.A.

TABLE OF CONTENTS

GOLF DIGEST BOOKS

EDITOR: JOHN R. MCDERMOTT

MANAGING EDITOR: DOUGLAS HARDY   SENIOR EDITOR: DWAYNE NETLAND

ASSISTANT EDITORS: ROBIN DAWSON, MARY MCPADDEN

DESIGN: RICHARD WARNER FOR LEONARD WOLFE DESIGN ASSOCIATES, INC.
DESIGN ASSISTANT: KONDYLO KATSARAKES

F O R E W O R D

I HAVE MANY WARM AND WONDERFUL THOUGHTS about Pebble Beach and the Carmel-Monterey Bay area. This glorious Peninsula holds a premier place in my memory bank just as it does within the game of golf in our country.

Perhaps my most poignant thought goes back to my college days and the chances I had to play golf there, usually on Saturday mornings before anybody else was on the course. I had been introduced to the starter, the late Ray Parga, by my father who knew him a long time ago. Ray was a very kind man and allowed me to play Pebble Beach for free. I used to drive down from Palo Alto when I was attending Stanford, leaving school before sunrise so I could be on the course by 6:30. I'd be first off, play the course without a single spike mark on the greens, and leave my dew prints on the moist, beautiful grass. I could set my own pace—which is pretty doggone quick today and was even quicker then. I played Pebble Beach many, many times in those days and it was always a thrill, always a beautiful sight and always stimulating to me as a person and a golfer.

I never shot good scores at that time, not like I did at other courses. I don't think I ever broke 73. But I do remember—and this is not just fabrication but solid fact—I used to pretend that I was neck and neck against Jack Nicklaus in the U.S. Open coming down to the wire on the last three holes at Pebble Beach. In 1982, of course, that college boy's daydream came true. As I stood on the 16th tee I had a one-shot lead over Jack as he was about to play the 71st and 72nd holes of our national championship. My drive found the deep right-fairway bunker and I proceeded to bogey and go into a tie with him. That set the stage for the most famous shot I have hit in golf and one of the greatest moments of my career. At the 17th, I pulled a 2-iron left of the pin. It was a bad situation. I faced a downhill chip from deep grass to a downhill green. The pin was no more than 15 to 16 feet away from me. My only legitimate play was to have the ball hit the pin, or else I was staring a devastating bogey in the face. I tried to hit the ball straight to the pin and, whoops, it went right down the hole. A birdie from a bad situation; a spot where 4 seemed more likely than 3, let alone 2. I almost jumped to the shores of Hawaii from the edge of the 17th green. Filled with emotion, I went on to birdie the last hole to win by two. It was my student days in real life; it was Pebble Beach and national television; it was Jack Nicklaus on the last three holes; it was the U.S. Open, a championship I had always wanted to win.

Another set of vivid thoughts involves the wonderful times I have spent watching and playing in the Bing Crosby (now the AT&T) National Pro-Am. My first memory of this Pebble Beach tradition was in the early '60s when I turned the TV to "the Crosby" and ABC came on with what I thought must be the Wide World of Sports downhill ski championship. But no, it was Pebble Beach in a blanket of snow. Weather, always the subject of conversation here, is as much a part of Monterey Peninsula golf as the eye-filling scenery. But I will never forget that telecast of the winds and the waves at the 18th hole.

Then in 1972, my second year on the tour, I qualified for the Crosby. It was such a thrill to be back playing a golf course I truly loved, one I consider to be among the great golf courses of the world. I have a host of memories playing Pebble Beach, especially winning the Crosby in 1977 and 1978. And I have enjoyed the two amateurs who have played here with me, Bob Willits and Sandy Tatum. They are fine players, great friends and wonderful people who truly reflect their love of this great game. A third—and very special—memory of the Pebble Beach area is quite recent. I was fortunate enough to be invited by Bobby Jones Jr., along with Sandy Tatum, to create a true links golf course on land the Pebble Beach Company has developed into The Links at Spanish Bay. Along with the Inn at Spanish Bay, I believe this is one of the great golf resorts in the world.

I've had lots of special feelings for this Peninsula. Not only do you see superb natural beauty here, but you smell it and sniff it. You breathe in the salty sea spray and the strange odors of the kelp beds, birds and sea life. Your ears can't help but pick up the crashing waves of the high seas or the quiet lapping of the evening surf. And my memory will ever retain the sound and the scent of that welcome fireplace at The Lodge at Pebble Beach after a round of golf.

And finally, there amid links of land, headland, woodland and the Pacific Ocean are those wonderful names: Spyglass Hill, Cypress Point, Stillwater Cove, Spanish Bay, Poppy Hills, Carmel-by-the-Sea, and, of course, Pebble Beach. I have special feelings here that I don't find elsewhere in the world, with the possible exception of a few special venues in Scotland at British Open time. But here at Pebble Beach one finds a perfect commune of golf, nature and man, important to the lives of all the people it touches, glorious to see and rich in memory to all who have played in its famous tournaments.

— *Tom Watson*

A PARADISE CALLED
PEBBLE BEACH

The Rugged Result of an Island That Moved

For centuries travelers have marveled at the exquisite natural beauty of the Monterey Peninsula. The white sand of Carmel's pristine beach, the jade-green pines above Monterey, the rare cypress trees of Del Monte Forest, the Santa Lucia Range crashing spectacularly into the Pacific, the granite edge of the cliffs, the unique offshore sea life and the warm pastoral scenery of Carmel Valley have all been held in wonderment by those who discover this unusual union of land and ocean.

Spanish explorer Juan Rodriguez Cabrillo discovered California for the Old World in 1542, sailing his two frigates north from Mexico. Returning from the Northwest Cape of California, he anchored on the night of November 18 off a rocky point named Cape San Martin (now called Point Pinos). His chronicle of the voyage, however, does not specifically record that he entered Monterey Bay. A Portuguese named Sebastian Rodriguez Cermeno was possibly first to enter the bay as he returned from the north in 1595.

It is widely accepted that the Spanish explorer Sebastian Vizcaino was the first European to step ashore at Monterey. In 1602 while mapping the area, Vizcaino noted that a special headland "appeared to be an island." Historians believe the headland was what we know today as Del Monte Forest, home to one of the most-revered golf resorts on earth, Pebble Beach. From aboard his sailing ship, the *San Diego*, Vizcaino could look northward to Pescadero Point and beyond to Point Pinos. To the south he could see

The Monterey Peninsula's coast testifies to ancient wars of water, fire and stone.

Carmel Mission in 1885. For more than two centuries, the mission founded by Father Serra has symbolized the Spanish history of Monterey. Now much expanded (see p. 133), its beautiful gardens still offer history and repose to visitors.

Point Lobos. Vizcaino named Monterey Bay to the north of the headland after his benefactor, Count de Monte Rey, who was then viceroy of New Spain. (The name means king's hill, or king's wood). Carmel, to the south, took its name from the nearby river, which three Carmelite friars from Vizcaino's voyage called "Rio Carmelo." The names, although translated and transformed, have been with us for nearly 400 years. On December 10, Vizcaino entered the bay and shortly thereafter he landed and conducted a ceremony under a live oak, taking posession of the land.

Writing with the imagination of an explorer hoping to make an indelible point for his followers, Vizcaino recorded all he saw in his journal and on his maps. He told of sheltered bays and coves, of pine trees suitable for masts, and of friendly natives; but for reasons history has not been able to fully explain no one followed Vizcaino to Monterey's shores for another 167 years. Perhaps he was overly enthusiastic in his descriptions and other explorers failed to recognize Vizcaino's discoveries or perhaps with the passage of time the Spanish had no need for a safe harbor at Monterey; whatever the reasons the Monterey Peninsula was to remain as Vizcaino had first seen it—an island unto itself.

The perception of the Monterey Peninsula as an "island" has persisted for years. Vizcaino was not the last to see this unique landform as an island; scientists have viewed the region as an ecological island for at least two centuries. Nearly 400 years after its discovery the Monterey Peninsula is still an island—at least psychologically—to those who live here and to many who visit here.

A MOVING ISLAND

During its geological development this region actually did take on the appearance of an island. In fact, there is geological evidence indicating the Santa Lucia Range, attaching itself to the Monterey Peninsula just to the south, was smaller during its formation and may have migrated north as an island.

In scientific time the Monterey Bay area began its development during the late Oligocene Epoch of the Tertiary Period. That makes it more than 25 million years old by the geological clock. Its origin began in southern California hundreds of miles to the south and its movement northward coincided with the activation of the San Andreas Fault.

As this huge "island" crept northward with each jerk of the San Andreas and lesser faults, the exposed portions gradually developed. This "coastal block," as geologists call it, included not only the Santa Lucia Range but also the Gabilans on the east side of the Salinas Valley, the Santa Cruz Range to the north of Monterey Bay and land formations as far north as Point Arena. Scientists stress, however, that they do not know exactly what the landscape looked like as it moved north. They do know, though, that the San Andreas Fault and its cross-faults continually changed the face of the earth's crust. These tectonic forces crumpled, shattered, elevated or depressed large land masses. Changes in sea level, eventual forces of erosion, greatly influenced the size and shape of the landscape.

During the millions of years that preceded the Great Ice Age earthquakes were common events, an inland sea covered the Salinas Valley, volcanoes formed and vanished, the Santa Lucia Range was elevated and the floor of Monterey Bay with its incredible submarine canyon continued to deepen. In effect, mountains and valleys were made and the bay was forming in its

A DINNERTIME LESSON ON MONTEREY'S PAST

Samuel F.B. Morse was fond of connecting the area's colorful history to his resort properties. During the 1930s he commissioned Joe Mora, a local artist and sculptor (known for his beautiful statue of Father Junipero Serra at the mission) to produce these historical covers for the Hotel Del Monte's dinner menus.

breadth and depth—all at an estimated northbound rate of 10 miles per one million years.

By the end of the Pliocene Epoch, or about two to five million years ago, the Santa Cruz Mountains lay just east of Monterey Bay and the Santa Lucia and Gabilan ranges were making their entrance at the southern boundary of the Monterey Peninsula. Volcanic action was dropping off, inland seas were subsiding and mountain streams were beginning their erosion process.

The Monterey Peninsula rides a complex series of geological fault lines, seen in the USGS map (below) *and in an infrared U-2 image of California's crumpled coastline* (left). *Pebble Beach Golf Links can be clearly seen—in red— at the lower right of the peninsula.*

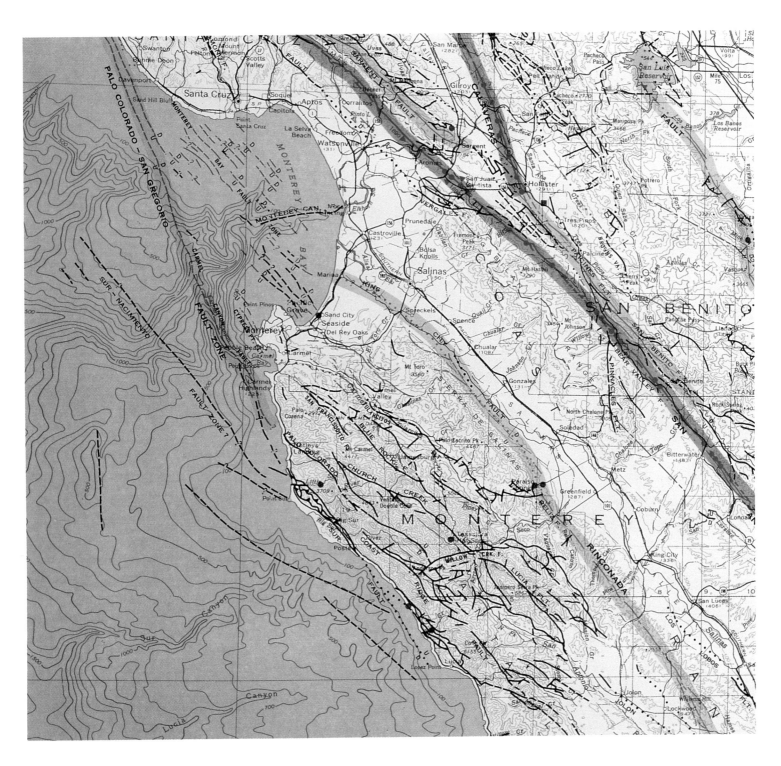

Climatic evolution was under way, and the Great Ice Age was coming.

The Great Ice Age began about three million years ago and its remnants still cover an estimated 10 percent of the Earth. At one time a gigantic ice sheet more than two miles thick covered the European Continent, the northern half of North America was under a layer of ice, much of the Sierra Nevada was buried in ice and valley glaciers on the west side inched down to about 4,000 feet. From this phenomenon, Yosemite Valley would be created.

Because of the vast area the Ice Age enveloped, there is a general belief that ice covered everything, but that isn't so. The Monterey Peninsula, like much of the California coastal environs, escaped the massive deep freeze. It was, however, subjected to various side effects of the glacial influence.

Sea levels changed as the formation of ice extracted water, and later, water returned as the ice melted. Mountain streams increased their paths of erosion when the sea level dropped, while simultaneously earthquakes, or tectonic activity, continued to raise the elevations of the Santa Lucia Range. As flat and rolling plains developed, the rising peaks of the Santa Lucia Range formed. At other times the sea and the land were both rising, although the land was rising at a faster pace. To make the scene even more complex, there were periods when the sea level was lowering and the land was sinking. The resulting erosion process was even more dramatic.

The Ice Age was now midway through its evolution and the Santa Lucia Range, periodically subjected to earthquakes on both its western and eastern slopes, was nearing its present location.

By compressing the passage of time, an unscientific luxury that brings us to the present, we know that during the last million years or so the sea

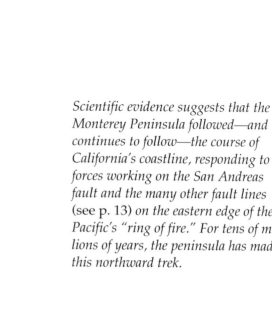

Scientific evidence suggests that the Monterey Peninsula followed—and continues to follow—the course of California's coastline, responding to forces working on the San Andreas fault and the many other fault lines (see p. 13) on the eastern edge of the Pacific's "ring of fire." For tens of millions of years, the peninsula has made this northward trek.

invaded and eventually retreated from the Salinas Valley. Monterey Bay and its environs continued to withdraw from the Santa Cruz Range to the north and the Santa Lucia Range to the south, terraces were formed, marine platforms were exposed, landslides blocked rivers and temporary lakes were formed and eventually the northward-bound "island" that began its trek somewhere off southern California in a much smaller form was to take the shape of the Monterey Peninsula.

FAULT ZONES

This is not to suggest the land is finally at rest. Anyone who has experienced even the mildest of earthquakes knows that geological change continues. The earlier rate of 10 miles traveled per million years is not particularly perceptible by today's standards for speed but it is inexorable.

The major fault zone in California is the San Andreas, which acted as the vehicle for bringing the Monterey Peninsula and its neighboring mountains and valleys to their present location. The San Andreas, located to the east, is not the only inland fault influencing the area. There is also the Sur-Nacimiento Fault Zone which crosses Monterey Bay. This fault zone is considered a "belt" of faults of various kinds and ages.

In the immediate region there are two other major fault zones off shore. These are the Palo Colorado-San Gregorio Fault Zone and the Monterey Bay Fault Zone.

Jose Cardero, an artist traveling in Monterey in 1791, sketched native peoples just before Europeans altered native life. This woman and man were probably of the Ohlone tribe.

Of most significance is the Palo Colorado-San Gregorio Fault Zone. By comparing this fault with the Hayward Fault in San Francisco's East Bay, scientists have theorized that it has the potential of creating an earthquake somewhere in the magnitude of 7.4 on the Richter scale.

The Palo Colorado-San Gregorio, although narrow, is nearly 100 miles in length and is seismically active. Dating back an estimated 300,000 to 500,000 years, it is to the south and southwest of the Monterey Peninsula and connects inland with the Palo Colorado fault south of Monterey and the San Gregorio fault at Ano Nuevo Point to the north. There is speculation that this fault zone, through interconnections with other faults, could be attached to the San Andreas Fault far to the north.

The other major fault zone is called Monterey Bay. Based on historical records of earthquakes dating back to 1836 it is known to be seismically active. An earthquake of magnitude 6.1 occurred in 1926 but the evi-

These ancient hand images, created by Esselen Indians of the Ohlone group, are the subject of Robinson Jeffers' poem, "Hands."

dence is hazy as to its epicenter being on the Monterey Bay Fault Zone or Palo Colorado-San Gregorio Zone. While the Palo Colorado-San Gregorio Fault Zone is less than two miles wide, the Monterey Bay Fault Zone is from six to nearly 10 miles wide and is on a trend with faults in the Salinas Valley. It is not known what magnitude earthquake it possesses but it includes a series of parallel faults extending northward from Cypress Point.

Within these two major fault zones there are numerous sizable faults that either parallel, overlap or crisscross the principal fault zones. Some of these faults undoubtedly played a part in the geological formation of the area. These include the Rinconada Fault, which runs through the Salinas Valley to the east; the Carmel Canyon Fault, just off shore; and faults along what is known as the Cypress Point-Point Sur shelf. The Cypress Point fault, for example, crosses Cypress Point and extends south through Pescadero Point which is not far from Pebble Beach's 18th hole.

Records going back to 1926 document that innumerable earthquakes with a range of 1.0 to 7.1 have occurred within this complex network. As more seismographs are installed and instrumentation becomes increasingly sensitive, earthquakes that once went undetected will now be recorded.

B 3874. CYPRESS POINT, MONTEREY.

WATKINS' NEW BOUDOIR SERIES, YO SEMITE AND PACIFIC COAST, 26 New Montgomery St., under Palace Hotel, S. F.

Postcards proved the striking setting to those back East long before this view (c. 1885) became hole No. 16 at Cypress Point Club.

Native Americans

When the Spaniard Vizcaino landed at Monterey and began to map his "island," he noted in his journal that the region was "thickly" populated. He wrote that the people were gentle, peaceful and even docile, generous and friendly. What he had witnessed was a European's first encounter with Native Americans of the central coast—in this instance, most probably the Ohlone Indians.

The Spanish called the Ohlone Indians "Costanoans," meaning coast people. Referred to today as Ohlone, they were a "linguistic" group that extended from San Francisco's Golden Gate region to Point Sur south of the Monterey Peninsula. The main dialectical subgroup living locally and as far as 10 to 15 miles up the Carmel Valley were the Rumsen. Two other Ohlone subgroups were the Mutsun, who lived in the San Juan Bautista area to the northeast and the Chalons in the Soledad region of the Salinas Valley.

In addition to the Ohlones there were the Salinan, who lived in the mid-to-southern portion of the Salinas Valley and along the South Coast to the San Luis Obispo county line, and the Esselen, who inhabited the upper watershed of the Carmel and Arroyo Seco Rivers and about 25 miles of the

Simple native tools such as bone awls (above) and arrowheads (below), *still found at Pebble Beach, indicate the importance of the area's early use as food-gathering territory.*

B 3882   GLIMPSE OF PEBBLE BEACH, CYPRESS DRIVE.   MONTEREY.
WATKINS' NEW BOUDOIR SERIES YO SEMITE AND PACIFIC COAST, 427 Montgomery Street, San Francisco.

A generation before it actually had a golf course, Pebble Beach's natural sweep shaped what would become Nos. 9 and 10.

coastal area south of Point Sur. The Salinan and Esselen Indians were also independent linguistic groups, different from the Ohlones. There are estimates that 7,500 to 10,000 Indians of all groups once lived within Monterey County, indicating that a much smaller population actually inhabited the Monterey Peninsula before the Catholic Mission era reached Monterey in 1770.

PEBBLE BEACH ARCHEOLOGICAL SITES

It was the dominating Rumsens and the Esselens to a lesser degree who left the imprint of their past for scientists to study today—the archeological site.

Archeological studies throughout the area, including a significant discovery in Pebble Beach in 1991, reveal that Del Monte Forest was inhabited by Indians as far back as 5,330 years ago, but little is known of that period. What is known, however, is that many of those important archeological sites lay protected and hidden from view under the Pebble Beach Golf Links.

The earliest known Indians built villages along the shores of Del Monte Forest and lived there regularly while later—perhaps hundreds or even thousands of years later—the Indians lived primarily inland and only came to Del Monte Forest to gather various shellfish. Today there are proven archeological sites at Spanish Bay, Cypress Point, Fanshell Beach, Pescadero Point, Stillwater Cove, and along the entire oceanside stretch of Pebble Beach Golf Links from the 18th tee box back to the 10th green, including the famous seventh hole at—appropriately enough—Arrowhead Point.

Samuel F.B. Morse wrote of his impressions of another spot which is presumed to have been a gathering place:

> The place that is locally known as the Indian Village is in the Del Monte Forest, just back of the high sand dunes, between the Monterey Peninsula Country Club and the Cypress Point golf links. There is a flat area in the Forest and quite a clearing … there is an active spring and a live pool of water at all seasons of the year. The oaks and pines grow to an especially large size along this creek and the clearing is bordered on all sides by a tall, straight pine forest with very little underbrush … .
>
> The legend of the place is that the Indians had used it as a sort of a cure; that when they were sick they came there to camp and that after they had stayed there a few days and taken of the waters of the spring they frequently felt better. … It is an interesting thing that [they] should have had a spa comparable with … Saratoga and Baden-Baden.

The Indians usually maintained two types of sites. One was the village and the other was the gathering station. Some sites were used for both purposes, although generations apart. Archeologists have been able to determine that after the Indians relocated inland they still returned to the shoreline to gather shellfish. To escape the wind, in this case at Spanish Bay, they would move under the trees where they built fires and cooked the shellfish. Discarding the shells at the site, the Indians would then return with the meat to their inland village.

Typical artifacts from these sites are spearheads, knife points, scrapers, and mortar and pestle fragments. Numerous shell beads, which were used like cash, indicated a site of economic importance. If there were no shell beads, the site was most probably a gathering location. Villages also revealed burial customs. Shell beads, for example, at a burial site spoke of the wealth of the dead. Fishing stations suggested nothing more than the Indians' interest in gathering shellfish which included such delicacies as abalone and mussels.

AN ECOLOGICAL ISLAND

The significance of a past culture at Pebble Beach goes far beyond the Indian's presence here; it unveils before us the natural environment that attracted humans to this locale 5,000 years ago and continues to do so to this day.

The ingredients for a near-perfect ecosystem have existed for hundreds of years on the Monterey Peninsula: a temperate climate, abundant food, unusual forms of plant life and vegetation, a varied landscape, and sea life and animals of all kinds. Some are common forms of life, others are only found in this area. Integrated as they are into a multifaceted network of wildlife, they combine to create a truly unique Peninsula. Ever since French scientist and navigator Jean Francois Galaup de la Perouse reported on Indian hunting methods in 1786, data has been gathered on the culture and natural history of the Monterey Peninsula. Geologists came here in 1861, phycologists in the late 1800s, pioneer botanists arrived in the early 1900s, and cypress tree counts began as early as 1921. Some scientists candidly admitted it was almost too much to comprehend, another labeled the area the "most important silva ever," and all agreed that taken as a whole there was nothing that compared with the Monterey Peninsula and especially Del Monte Forest.

What attracted them was not just the obvious natural beauty of the area, but the plant and animal life that it contained. Within Del Monte Forest

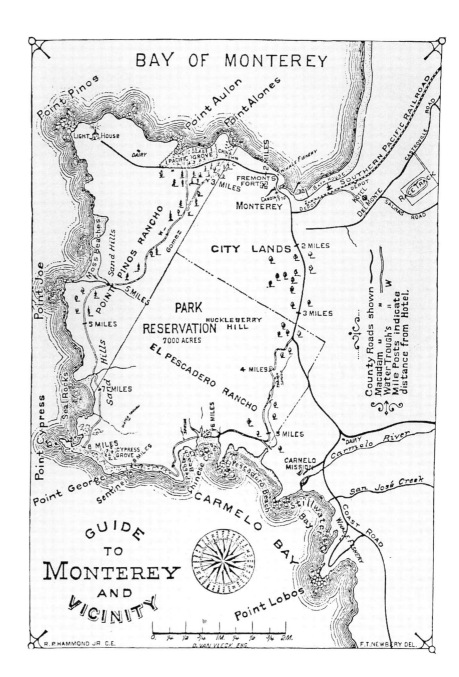

Guests at the Hotel Del Monte in the 1910s could use this map of the 17-Mile Drive to find their way down dirt and macadam roads to the popular picnic spot called Pebble Beach.

BACK WHEN THE LAWNMOWERS WORE WOOL

The extraordinary beauty of Pebble Beach may appear to be much the same as it has always been but there remains a presence of what has come and gone—the recording of Pebble Beach's history, as in these photographs, is proof of that.

Rare Tule Elk *(upper left)*, transplanted to this forested land as a preservation effort in 1914, were safely moved to other regions of California 23 years later when they outgrew their range. In 1890 a family of three half-breed buffalo *(upper right)* was kept at a private zoological garden in Pebble Beach, and in 1920 a herd of 300 sheep *(below)* was temporarily used to "mow" the young golf course.

In more modern times, a mined-out sand plant site became a restored dunes habitat and golf course, unusual native plants and trees have been identified and protected and vast shorelines dedicated to open space.

Rich in such natural resources, Pebble Beach has always been a guarded reserve of various preservation efforts, which in turn have made their individual and unique imprints on history—fleeting though they may have been.

there are more than 100 vascular plants, over 30 plants that grow only near the ocean, more than 200 different birds and three types of exceptionally unusual trees that grow no where else in the world.

Because of the climate-soil-locale combination, the stunted Gowen Cypress and Bishop Pine can be found only in Del Monte Forest. Their stunted, or dwarf, form is a result of the sterile, acid-type soil in which they grow. They are particularly rare because they grow successfully in the immediate company of the Monterey Pine and do not hybridize. In effect, the species remain isolated and distinct. Just as rare is the Monterey Cypress, easily the most photographed symbol of Del Monte Forest. There is also the rare Bear-Grass and Mock-Heather.

Del Monte Forest, which rises from sea level to 800 feet above sea level, is an area of not only forest, but canyons, sand dunes and shoreline. Because of its unusual topography the floral areas also shelter rare plant life. In addition to the Gowen Cypress, Bishop Pine and Monterey Pine the forest areas contain Scouler's Willow, wild Douglas Iris, Slender Rein Orchids and Alaska Rein Orchids. The canyons harbor various ferns, Alum-Root and Huckleberry, the red Pine Rose and the pink Wood Rose. Sand dunes are home to the endemic Beach Monkey-Flower, both the Pink and Yellow San-Verbena, Bush Lupine and Beach Morning-Glory. At the shoreline, clinging to the rocks, snuggled into the cliffs, or growing on the open mesas are California Beach Poppies, Goldfields, blue Sky Lupine and the lavender Seaside Daisy.

The fractured granite coast is a special habitat for animals, whether they are carnivores, herbivores or omnivores. There are black-tailed coastal deer, raccoons, rabbits and a variety of small nocturnal animals. Once a herd of Tule Elk was transplanted to Del Monte Forest as a preservation measure, but they proved to be one of the few species that did not adapt and in 1922 they were shipped to northern California. It has been rumored, however, that some elk still roam the hot and rugged Santa Lucia Mountains near San Simeon and Hearst Castle—far from Del Monte Forest.

Because archeological evidence only goes back a mere 5,000 years on the Monterey Peninsula, it is not known if camels, saber-toothed tigers, wolves, ancient horses and mammoths, which were common to the north and south of the central coast during this period, also lived here. Animal life 5,000

Its isolation has made the Monterey Peninsula home to a number of unique plant species, some endangered. From top right, the Gowan Cypress begins life; the Bishop Pine cone survives harsh conditions; the nuts and foliage of a mature Gowan Cypress, which grows only in two locations; and the more common seaside daisy at Cypress Point.

LIFE ON THE EDGE

Despite the violence of crashing waves, a rich variety of life thrives in the tidal areas. Stars of the show, and the amateur photographer's delight, are the area's harbor seals.

In its ecological makeup and importance, the Del Monte Forest is as much ocean as it is land.

One of the first impressions visitors have as they enter 17-Mile Drive is the expanse of the Pacific Ocean and its visual impact. Here, nature has created a force unlike any other on earth.

Winter waves crash violently against offshore rocks and onto the durable shoulders of broad beaches. Seagulls, pelicans and cormorants skim through the misty air. In summer months the ocean sometimes lies flat and still, engulfed in fog or basking under brilliant blue skies. The sea life is at peace, too, as harbor seals float offshore watching the visitors watch them, or playful sea otters, keeping time with the rhythmic ebb of the ocean, bob up and down on kelp beds.

Closer to shore is the intertidal zone or, more commonly, the tide pools. Depending on the direction of the tide, the tide pools are relatively safe little exhibits of the miniature forms of sea life that exist in the ocean. The pools offer a mind-

boggling view of life under the ocean's surface.

Along 17-Mile Drive are turnouts leading to photo opportunities at Cypress Point, Fanshell Beach, Seal Rock, Bird Rock, Point Joe, Moss Beach and Spanish Bay. But a word of warning: The seals and birds don't read the signs and don't distinguish between Seal Rock and Bird Rock.

At Cypress Point look for the light-colored, large Steller sea lion. Typically, bulls and young females are seen there but most older sea lions stay farther south at Point Lobos.

The barking noise at Bird Rock is a giveaway that despite its name the rock's main tenants are the dark-colored California sea lions. The creatures do "nest" but in late June they head south for breeding season. The higher tips of Bird Rock are home for nesting pairs of Brandt's cormorants.

Of course, birds of varying species are seen along the entire shoreline of Pebble Beach. They range from numerous species of gulls, including the "local" Western gull, to the belted kingfisher, to the near-mythical blackfooted albatross.

Newborn harbor seals can be seen during April and May feeding, basking and, after venturing out, keeping in touch with Mom.

Ed Ricketts (above), *a marine biologist and friend of John Steinbeck, was the model for "Doc" in the novel* Cannery Row. *Nick Nolte* (below) *appeared more glamorous as Ricketts in Hollywood's version of the book.*

years ago was much the same as it is today with the exception that the grizzly bear is gone from the scene and wild boar, turkeys and Virginia possums have been imported.

Tide pools are an adventure for both the scientists and the amateur, and the study of intertidal life has never been the same since Ed Ricketts and Jack Calvin wrote *Between Pacific Tides* in 1939. Ricketts, who collected from the area's intertidal zone and studied his specimens at his Cannery Row lab, became the fictionalized "Doc" in John Steinbeck's classic *Cannery Row*. More than one romantically inclined youth has fallen under the influence of Ricketts and become a marine biologist. And why not? The Pebble Beach intertidal zone is rich in marine life. The tide pools along Point Joe, Bird Rock, Fan Shell Beach and Pescadero Point are a marine biologist's paradise. At various tide levels there are periwinkle snails hiding between rocks, limpets and barnacles, snails, small crabs, sea anemones and hermit crabs. Deep within the outer reaches of the tidal zone are sponges, little abalones, sea stars and sea urchins.

Another form of life in the tidal zone is marine algae. Along the shoreline of Del Monte Forest there are an estimated 200 species, including 15 types that are not found anywhere else in the world. Contributing to this extremely delicate environment is a mixture of rocks covered by the shifting fine sand.

The Pebble Beach shoreline is also the vantage point for experiencing other forms of life—the passing parade of whales, dolphins, porpoises and countless other sea creatures.

The most difficult to observe from shore are members of the dolphin and porpoise family, but the killer whale with its six-foot high dorsal fin cannot be mistaken, nor can one mistake the California Gray Whale on its 6,000-mile migration from the frigid North Bering Sea to the warm lagoons of Baja California where its calves are born. The southern migration, when the gray whales are close to shore, is from late November through February. Their migration north is in March and April.

Point Joe on the north side of the peninsula is one of three locations on the California coast where great white sharks have been spotted.

Resident sea otters, once thought to be extinct, are now commonplace in the kelp beds of Point Lobos, Carmel Bay and off Del Monte Forest. The sea otter is the little guy floating on his back, cracking a shell on his stomach. Northern elephant seals arrive at Del Monte Forest beaches during their spring molt and the year-round California sea lions can be found at Bird Rock, of all places, off 17-Mile Drive. Steller sea lions are off Cypress Point in May and harbor seals or "leopard seals" are appropriately seen on Seal Rock, which is also found along 17-Mile Drive, in April and May when their young are nursed. Fanshell Beach is a major seal birthing area.

Considering its unique beauty and abundant life there can be no doubt why the early Indians chose to make their home along the shores of Pebble Beach or why scientists have been studying the area for more than 200 years. The natural habitat seen in Del Monte Forest now is still much the same as the Indians saw it thousands of years ago and when the first Europeans mapped its bays and hills in 1602.

PRESERVING THE LAND

Today there are 5,300 acres within Del Monte Forest. Of that total Pebble Beach Company owns more than half, or over 3,500 acres. Through careful planning and under the management of its preservation-minded founder Samuel F.B. Morse private homes have been built and golf courses created. The change has been thoughtful and gradual, out of respect for the history and fragile nature of the land.

That's as it should be. And to reinforce that respect for rare and unusual plants and animal life—and in honor of the natural beauty of the land—many areas of Del Monte Forest have been protected by ordinance as preserves and permanent open space.

The golf courses, for example, are deemed open space in perpetuity.

The annual monarch butterfly migration drapes area trees with flowing capes of orange and black.

THE LONE CYPRESS

Standing sentinel on a granite outcropping at Midway Point the Lone Cypress is one of the most famous and most photographed trees in the world.

Its facsimile has been the registered trademark and corporate logo of Pebble Beach Company since 1935 because it is a living expression of nature's complex makeup—in Del Monte Forest, the ocean and the area's rugged shoreline.

Only in Del Monte Forest and at Point Lobos does the Monterey Cypress grow in its natural state and only at Pebble Beach has such a magnificent tree carved out such a precarious perch above the Pacific. Although it survived on its own for countless years the tree now has help.

Access to the tree has been eliminated because of damage people inflicted on it in the past. Even something as seemingly insignificant as foot traffic compacted the soil and prevented oxygen and water from reaching the roots. Now visitors in cars, busses and on bicycles stop at a small parking area nearby and descend steps to an observation point. No first-time observer remains unmoved by the tree's solitary stand against the Pacific elements.

Each November fertilizer is injected into the soil around the tree's perimeter. Support cables to safeguard against natural damage are checked regularly. Rainfall determines watering.

It is estimated that the Lone Cypress has withstood the relentless Pacific for nearly 250 years and with the care it receives, it should live to be over 300 years old. Experts say the tree could remain standing another 300 years after it dies because the wood is so dense.

Together, the courses owned by Pebble Beach Company—Pebble Beach Golf Links, Spyglass Hill Golf Course, Peter Hay Golf Course and The Links at Spanish Bay—total 460 acres of open space. Spanish Bay, built on the site of a former silica-sand mining operation, is of particular significance because it includes a large area of restored dune habitat that is not part of the actual course. Some golf courses located on the peninsula which are not owned by the Pebble Beach Company—Cypress Point Club, Poppy Hills Golf Course and Monterey Peninsula Country Club and its two courses—contribute another 740 acres to the overall open space of Del Monte Forest.

The regions where rare plant life exists, such as the stands of Gowen Cypress and Bishop Pine, are also protected. Nearly 200 acres of this delicate environment is in the process of being transferred to the Del Monte Forest Foundation, a separate entity responsible for the management and guidance

The natural—and also manmade—environment at Spanish Bay reflects unforgettable sunsets from the Pacific through the pines that line the links.

Many Peninsula residents contribute to the care and feeding of their neighbors, sometimes bringing the sushi *bar down to the local sea otter pup.*

of special reserves in Del Monte Forest. There are seven of these reserves totaling another 200 acres, including the famous Crocker Grove, the Pescadero Vista Point and the S.F.B. Morse Botanical Reserve.

In all there are an estimated 1,600 acres within Del Monte Forest that are under the protection of open space or habitat reserve. Of these, more than 800 acres are under the stewardship of Pebble Beach Company or Del Monte Forest Foundation.

In years to come more land will be dedicated as open space, assuring future visitors to this area that they will behold what others have before them—a natural setting worthy of unlimited praise.

For this is a land that had its beginnings more than 25 million years ago, a land that has historically been honored by its occupants; an extraordinary land by any comparison, a land that has slowly evolved into its modern form.

Evolution, as gradual as it may be, brings change. A new era arrived here shortly after the turn of this century and with it there was a new beginning—a beginning that can be traced to the arrival of S.F.B. Morse.

The Majesty of Monterey

There is something about water that makes people want to listen to and watch it forever. But at Pebble Beach the timpani of crashing surf and the quieter strings—the Pacific washing up on a beach with real pebbles—are only a small part of the peninsula's breathtaking symphony. Here and on the pages following we take you on a picture tour of the flora and fauna of Monterey that make up nature's most extraordinary concert.

A gray whale sounding on its annual journey south, and thunder on the rocks below the famous Lone Cypress set the mood for the spectacle.

Monterey's Air Force: a Familiar and Hardy Breed

At top, a flock of ruddy turnstones head for a beach and a place to feed. Above, a group of Canada geese, not a golfer's delight, graze on Pebble Beach's 9th hole. Above right, the ubiquitous brown pelican dares you to observe the sign. On facing page, Bird Rock, one of 17-Mile Drive's best photo ops, is home to pelicans and cormorants.

If there's anything the sea otter (left) is not, it's camera-shy. Above, a group of male California sea lions, yearlings and juveniles, bask on their favorite rock formation. At right, Pacific black-tail deer graze on the links, oblivious to golfers playing through. These herbivores play havoc with local gardens. Below, a band of midnight garbage collectors begin their rounds.

A Floral Freeway for the Bugs and Birds

Pacific Grove's coastline is illuminated during the day by ice plant (left). Meanwhile Monarch butterflies flit their way among Pride of Madeira plants (below) and, above, a ladybug inspects a yarrow plant during its daylong rush hour. At right, kelp torn from the ocean floor harbors tiny crabs, sand fleas and other culinary delights for area birds. Bottom pictures show more iceplant (left), yellow tar weed (center) and more Pride of Madeira.

A Mind-boggling Floor Show, Down in the Deep

The peninsula is a living kaleidascope for skindivers. At far left, top to bottom: a chiton, a sea star and a group of yellow sponges. At left, strawberry anemones at 50 feet. Below, a forest of kelp is home to smaller fish. At right, a sea anemone in a Pebble Beach tidal pool; a brittle starfish on compound tunicate; and ochre starfish at 65 feet.

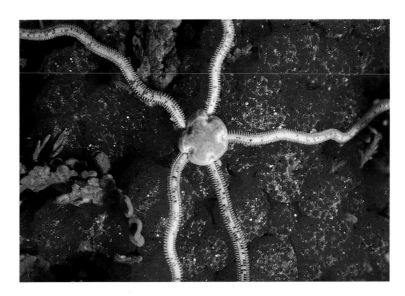

When the surf's up
It's a good time
For a light show

Although the California drought has
curtailed rainbows elsewhere, Monterey
has good luck producing arcs that last
from 10 to 15 minutes.

"He had imagination, humor, courage and a song in his heart."
— GENE TUNNEY, undefeated heavyweight boxing
champion, in remembrance of S.F.B. Morse after
learning of his death in 1969.

The Duke and His Stunning Realm

The Monterey Peninsula is home to an unmatched collection of resorts, golf courses, and natural spaces, and the sites operated by the Pebble Beach Company amount to a Peninsula-wide recreational paradise. That is the culmination of a dream fostered by one man, who came to the Peninsula in the early part of this century. Samuel Finley Breese Morse found here the beginnings of a real estate and resort business—after a century and a half of Monterey's development, begun by the Spanish.

Samuel F.B. Morse in 1926. The "Duke of Del Monte" promoted special Lodge events and spread the gospel on tinted postcards.

Crowds gathered around the 10-year-old Lodge at the 1929 U.S. Amateur Championship (left). Below, the post-card version of the Lodge.

For 250 years after its discovery by Spanish explorer Sebastian Vizcaino the Monterey Peninsula was the power base for all social, political, religious and commercial decisions made in California.

It began with the persistence of Gaspar de Portola, commander of Spain's land expeditions to explore Alta California in the second half of the eighteenth century. Moving north from Mexico, de Portola passed through Monterey in 1770 and "rediscovered" the safe harbor that Vizcaino had described in 1602. By prearrangement, Father Junipero Serra, Spain's president of the California missions, arrived in Monterey a week after Portola. Father Serra, a Spanish Franciscian who had gone to Mexico to do missionary work among the native peoples, had the previous summer founded Mission San Diego, the first of the missions in what is now California. When Father Serra said mass on June 3, 1770 under the same live oak where Vizcaino had held his ceremony of possession Monterey was officially founded and the Mission San Carlos was established that year.

Under Junipero Serra the Monterey Peninsula was the seat of mission authority. It was from here that he conducted the establishment of Catholic missions throughout the state, including moving his mission headquarters to San Carlos de Borromeos, which is more commonly known today as Carmel Mission.

Father Serra lived and worked at his Carmel Mission for nearly 14 years until his death in 1784 at the age of 71. He was beatified in 1988 and is buried at the Carmel Mission.

Monterey became the capital of Alta California, then Alta and Baja California, and ultimately the seat of the California Constitutional convention, a prelude to California's becoming the 31st state of the union. In its years as a governing township the flags of three countries were raised over Monterey—Spain, the Mexican Empire and the United States.

Another Spaniard was also influential in the early establishment of Monterey—albeit in a different way. He was Juan Bautista de Anza. After first seeing Monterey in 1774 de Anza returned two years later leading a remarkable expedition of men, women and children and hundreds of cattle and horses from Mexico. It was de Anza who was most responsible at the time for colonizing Monterey.

The mission authority in California continued for almost four decades after Fr. Serra's death but it was in gradual decline. In 1821, after 300 years of Spanish rule, Mexico became an independent country, and with its new freedom Mexico reclaimed most of the mission lands and formed them into huge California land grants under private ownership. The Spanish embargo on foreign trade was lifted, cattle became a chief commodity and the Spanish rule came to an end.

The Mexican Empire flag was raised in Monterey in 1822 and remained there—off and on—for 24 years. It was temporarily lowered in 1842 due to what might be called a military misunderstanding.

Commodore Thomas ap Catesby Jones, under the mistaken impression

Juan Bautista de Anza brought the first group of outside visitors to the Monterey Peninsula—240 men and women. The expedition continued north to found San Francisco.

that the United States was at war with Mexico, led a bloodless attack on the town of Monterey from the sea and prompted the surrender of Governor Juan Bautista Alvarado. The Stars and Stripes were raised in victory but not for long. Within a few hours Jones discovered his mistake. He apologized to Governor Alvarado, the Americans withdrew and the Mexican flag was raised once again.

Four years later, in 1846, the U.S. and Mexico were in fact at war and this time Commodore John Drake Sloat led troops ashore in another bloodless attack on Monterey. The Mexican flag was again lowered and permanently replaced by the Stars and Stripes. (Commodore Thomas ap Catesby Jones was eventually cleared of misconduct and given a new command.)

With one false start as a preface, Monterey and the rest of California became the property of the United States.

When the United States flag was raised permanently over Monterey in 1846 three Americans stood ready to assume influential roles in the development of the new territory.

Their names—Thomas Oliver Larkin, Walter Colton and Rev. Robert Semple—found their way into California history and today, across the entrances to many of the state's public schools. Unknown to one another before they met in Monterey they shared a common fervor for having California annexed by the United States and eventually becoming a state.

Larkin was the first to arrive. Like S.F.B. Morse generations later he was a Yankee. A merchant from Boston, he came to Monterey in 1832 with the intention of milling flour. Instead he became the U.S. Consul to Mexico in 1843, an appointment made by President John Tyler. In 1845 President James K. Polk made him a secret government agent to ensure that nothing upset the United States' intention of taking over California.

Colton, chaplain of the frigate U.S.S. Congress, sailed into Monterey July 15, 1846, just eight days after the Sloat conquest. Sloat's successor, Commodore Robert F. Stockton, appointed Monterey's first alcalde, a sort of mayor, but with executive, legislative and judicial authority.

Semple was a pioneer from Kentucky right down to his coonskin hat. He rose to prominence as a leader of the Bear Flag Revolt, the Sonoma rebellion against Mexican rule, less than a month before Sloat's takeover of Monterey. Semple traveled to Monterey and within three years he was named the president of the California Constitutional convention.

Monterey was now occupied by U.S. military forces. Larkin, Colton and Semple were civilians but one Army officer stationed at Monterey from 1847 to 1849 who went on to make a name for himself was Lt. William Tecumseh Sherman. Sixteen years later, Sherman would become famous as a general in the Civil War. Sherman's Monterey headquarters was in a small house behind Larkin's home and consul office where Colton, as alcalde, also had an office.

Larkin, Colton and Semple were to formally unite in late 1849 at the California constitutional convention held at Colton Hall in Monterey.

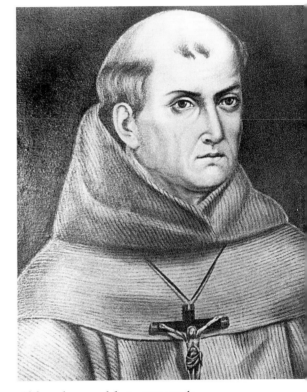

Although some debate surrounds Fr. Junepero Serra's work among native peoples, his mission undeniably attracted other Europeans to Monterey.

(Colton had built the convention site as a school but over the years it provided various uses). The three men, with Semple leading the convention, joined delegates from all over California in drafting a constitution.

The signing of the constitution was celebrated with a 31-gun salute. Though intended to mark a great beginning the salute also marked the apex of Monterey's predominence in the affairs of what was to become the largest state in the Union. The following year, on Sept. 9, 1850, California was admitted to the union. Gold had been discovered in the north near Sacramento and Monterey's influence over the social, political, religious and commercial life of California was coming to an end.

In its early years the Monterey Peninsula attracted explorers, pioneers, settlers and entrepreneurs of varying sorts and character—all seeking new lives, futures and in some cases, fortunes.

Midway through the 19th century, however, newcomers began to look at the Monterey Peninsula differently from their predecessors. Monterey had grown from a sleepy Spanish settlement to become the most important town in California's young history but statehood, the growing influence of other areas such as San Francisco and the swelling population in the north during

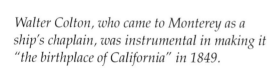

Walter Colton, who came to Monterey as a ship's chaplain, was instrumental in making it "the birthplace of California" in 1849.

the gold rush of 1849 eventually eroded Monterey's influence.

In 1850, the year California became the 31st state, Walter Colton and Robert Semple began publishing the first newspaper in California. It was a weekly printed on cigarette paper and they called it, rightfully, *The Californian*. A newspaper was certainly a sign that stability was arriving in an ever-changing Monterey. That same year a Scotsman named David Jacks came to Monterey. Crafty in his land dealings—so crafty, in fact, that he was widely disliked—Jacks became the richest man in Monterey County with an original investment of $4,000. At one Mexican land grant auction, for example, he bought 30,000 acres of land that had been owned by the City of Monterey for $1,000. Gradually he amassed over 60,000 acres.

The community's dislike for Jacks even attracted the attention of a fellow Scot, Robert Louis Stevenson, in 1879 when the future author of *Treasure Island* and *Strange Case of Dr. Jekyll and Mr. Hyde* stopped in Monterey for 3 $\frac{1}{2}$ months during his pursuit of Fanny Osbourne. Stevenson spent his 29th birthday in Monterey but an unfortunate brush fire, which many believed he had carelessly set, caused Stevenson to become unwelcome as well. He returned hastily to San Francisco.

Explorer, adventurer and sometime senator John C. Frémont used his leadership of California militia, including a foray with fellow adventurer Kit Carson into Monterey, to launch his political career.

In the 1890s the Del Monte station welcomed the gentry of San Francisco and Sacramento to the Peninsula.

Among the visitors: a lovesick R.L. Stevenson...

... whose modest dwelling was vacated in a hurry.

Perhaps to counter public opinion Jacks later donated land for the establishment of the Methodist Retreat, which became Pacific Grove. His heirs also made significant donations of landmark buildings and park sites.

Importantly for the history of Pebble Beach Jacks sold 7,000 acres to the Pacific Improvement Company in 1879. That acreage included Monterey beachfront property and portions of Del Monte Forest.

When Charles Crocker of the "Big Four" railroad empire arrived in Monterey that year a narrow-gauge railroad was serving Monterey from the Salinas Valley. With Crocker's lead Southern Pacific acquired the narrow gauge right-of-way and converted it into a standard railroad. Crocker liked what he saw in Monterey and believed that the land the Pacific Improvement Company owned could be the core of a new direction for Monterey. Crocker saw the Monterey Peninsula as the fashion spa of the future and a railroad was the best way for people to travel south from San Francisco and San Jose. As the 19th century was in its final quarter, tourism was about to become the new business of Monterey.

The scenery was breathtaking, the climate sublime. All Monterey needed, Crocker thought, was something to draw people accustomed to comfort. The enticement Crocker devised to draw customers from the cities to the north was the original Hotel Del Monte. Built in 1880, it became the magnet that drew high society to the Monterey Peninsula.

Thirty-five years later the Hotel Del Monte was being managed by a forceful young New Englander. S.F.B. Morse arrived in Monterey as its new role of resort was about to be reborn.

"... *while you thought of no one, nearly half a world away/ Someone thought of Louis on the beach of Monterey!" (from* A Child's Garden of Verses)

On a summer day in 1968, Samuel F.B. Morse walked into the intimate, white-carpeted, executive offices of the Del Monte Properties Company, making a point of saying good morning to each member of his immediate staff before going to his own office.

Typically, he was wearing a tweed sport coat, dress shirt with bow tie, pleated trousers and brown loafers. He walked with only the slight use of a thick-handled cane. Outside, at the curb, was his 1966 red Mustang coupe. On its grille was a Del Monte Forest emblem bearing the number "1."

He was Yale, class of '07, captain of the national collegiate championship football team—literally a gentleman of the old school—who had been transplanted as a young entrepreneur to the western edge of the continent. And on this day he was 82.

"Where's Otis?" His voice boomed from the inner sanctum of his private office. "Has anybody seen Otis?" Otis was the company's chief forester, charged with keeping Del Monte Forest in prime condition. "Well, when you see him, tell him to stop planting those trees in straight lines. Forests don't grow in straight lines." The order was meant for his personal secretary, but everyone within earshot got the message. S.F.B. (Sam) Morse, founder of Pebble Beach, known the world over to statesmen, politicians and movie stars as the "Duke of Del Monte" had a right to his proprietary interest in

Morse, grandnephew and namesake of the telegraph's inventor (above), was bred an Eastern gentleman, including a 1906 stint as the Yale football captain.

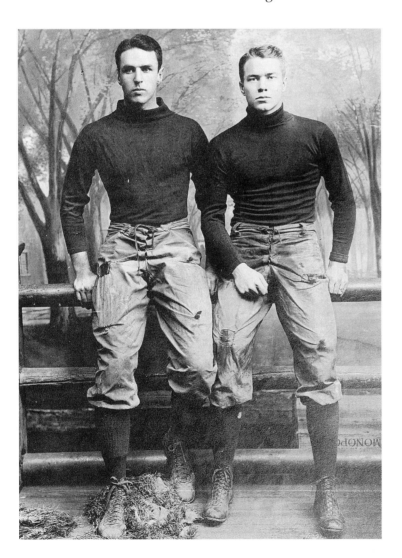

the forest. With nature's help Morse had, with incredible insight and foresight, created within that forest the finest golf resort on earth.

His work had been a labor of love; a love for the beauty of the trees, the cliffs, the ocean, and a love for seizing the challenge in front of him. Morse was, after all, "the grand old man of American business." It had taken some time to achieve such a distinction even if he was the grandnephew of S.F.B. Morse, the inventor and artist.

Morse had first arrived at Pebble Beach 60 years earlier. The year was 1908 and he, his wife and baby son were there because of William H. Crocker, uncle of Templeton Crocker who had been a year behind Morse at Yale. Crocker had recently hired Morse to manage a 40,000-acre ranch the Crocker-Huffman Company owned in California's San Joaquin Valley. Morse had landed the job on the strength of an on-site report he had made of the ranch's cattle and irrigation programs.

On that summer day Crocker was hosting a picnic on ground that is now the most famous finishing hole in golf. But at that time there were few homes and the land was used mostly for grazing cattle and for outings by guests of the Hotel Del Monte in Monterey. The original 17-Mile Drive was in place but a simple wooden lodge without guest rooms wouldn't be added until about 1909. And it would be 11 years before a golf course would be built there. The land was held by the Pacific Improvement Company in which the Crockers had an interest.

Before joining Crocker Morse had worked briefly for John Hayes Hammond, a mining engineer who owned the Mt. Whitney Power Company in Visalia, Calif. Most importantly for the ultimate advancement of young Morse, Hammond was an ardent Yale man. Morse, who later joked that Hammond "apparently thought that a successful football captain could do anything," was charged with going to California and determining if there was land to be bought and sold for a profit, based on the availability of Hammond's electrical power.

Born in Newtonville, which was part of Newton, Mass., on July 19, 1885, Morse had been to Paris twice with his family by the time he was 4. But those early sojourns had hardly left an indelible impression on him. Now he was just 22, and not only had he never been to California, the only other time he had ever been out of New England was to attend an Army-Navy football game in Pennsylvania. He was the first to admit that he knew nothing about land in any form outside New England.

"Up until I went West I thought Buffalo was in the far west and Chicago was some sort of oasis in the great western plains," Morse once said.

There was nothing, however, keeping Morse in the East. When he was a sophomore at Yale his father died in Marseille, France during an around-the-world trip. Now, out of college, Morse wanted to go to what he considered "far-flung" places. California in 1907 was certainly that.

When John Hayes Hammond's newest employee got off the train in Visalia he wasn't ready for the hot San Joaquin Valley town. To S.F.B. Morse, a Bostonian with a Yale degree, Visalia turned out to be a dismal destination. There were dirt streets, elevated sidewalks, hitching posts everywhere, few cars and many saloons. This area of California, miles from large cities and their amenities, looked more like a wild west setting than a promising business destination. Nearby, however, lay Monterey and the Pacific Improvement Company.

On a hefty salary of $300 a month he rented a house and hired a Chinese cook. He also had a trust fund that earned him almost $1,000 a year.

It's safe to say he never looked back. Well, perhaps once. As Hammond's representative Morse purchased about 4,000 acres at $35 each near Delano and drilled the first irrigation wells in that area. It soon became apparent the venture would not turn a profit and Morse returned East to give Hammond his report and his resignation. It was during the time they would call The Panic of 1907. A drop in the stock market had caused a brief depression and J. Pierpont Morgan, the country's leading financier, was called on to arrange foreign lending. Europe sent $100 million in gold and the U.S. economy was restored. But for the first and only time in his adult life, Morse was without a job. And ill.

Unaccountably he had picked up amoebic dysentery and had to undergo three major operations for a perforated intestine and a liver abscess. It took all his savings. When William H. Crocker hired him to return to the hot San Joaquin Valley Morse was trying to get a job on newspapers drawing cartoons. He was to spend eight years in the valley and they were eight years of continuous success within the Crocker organization.

In April, 1915 Crocker was to lend his influence once again. The Crocker estate owned an interest in the Pacific Improvement Company (P.I.), and Morse was asked to manage it. P.I. had been the holding

Even as an adopted Californian Morse's style and élan reflected his cosmopolitan tastes, including a different kind of captaincy.

company for the Central and Southern Pacific Railroads but P.I. and the railroads had parted and stock in the railroads had been sold off. Now the former holding company controlled town sites, ranches, resorts, timberlands and coal mines across the country and into Central America. Among these holdings was the "Del Monte unit." It was this segment of P.I.'s vast enterprise that Morse was to oversee. He was 29.

The "Del Monte unit" was significant in itself, consisting of the Hotel Del Monte with its leased-land golf course, a polo field, racetrack and beach property; the undeveloped 5,300-acre Del Monte Forest; The Monterey County Water Works, which supplied water to Monterey, Carmel and Pacific Grove; an expansive cattle ranch in Carmel Valley; and extensive ocean frontage in Pacific Grove and another hotel located on that town's main business street.

The Monterey Peninsula could have been a "company town" of gigantic proportions but that was not P.I.'s interest nor Morse's goal.

Identifiable today are such former P.I. holdings as the Hotel Del Monte, now the Naval Postgraduate School; the polo grounds with 350 stalls, three tournament fields, various practice areas and mile-long race track and

President Theodore Roosevelt stopped at the Hotel Del Monte in 1903. He wrote to his young son back East that he wished they could enjoy the outdoor life in Monterey together, riding, hunting and exploring the magnificent shoreline (presumably Pebble Beach, along some of the riding routes the President took).

steeplechase course, now a Navy golf course; hundreds of undeveloped home sites in Pacific Grove, now a municipal 18-hole golf course with bordering residential neighborhoods; undeveloped land that is now the site of the Monterey Peninsula Airport and Del Monte Research Park; prime property that is now the Del Monte Shopping Center; valuable "view" land that is now the site of the Monterey Peninsula Community Hospital; land known as the "Old Capitol Site" in Monterey, now proposed for a hospice center; even the Del Monte Laundry, now privately owned.

In Carmel Valley there were equally vast and influential holdings. There was the 12,000-acre Los Laureles cattle ranch, once a Mexican land grant and since divided into various smaller parcels, including Los Laureles Lodge which was the original ranch house; the 2,500-acre Monterey County Water Company which held majority water rights and built the San Clemente Dam on the Carmel River; and the River Ranch which was Morse's personal retreat and remains in the family. In all there were an estimated 20,000 acres, of which 12,000 acres were in Carmel Valley.

By today's standards, the "Del Monte unit" was not only strategically located to benefit from future growth, it was immeasurably valuable. There

Morse's college friend Templeton Crocker (above) *was a key connection to the western gentry* (below, at a picnic near Pebble Beach).

Just after the turn of the century, the original log Lodge (right) provided a rustic change from such luxuries as the Del Monte Bath House (below).

was a railroad, a hotel and golf course, land at the beach, land in the valley, land on the mountains and all importantly—water. But that is a late 20th-century concept not 1915 reality. Implausible as it may seem in retrospect, most of the "Del Monte unit" was losing money.

Morse's assignment: liquidate.

Unfortunately, P.I. had already sold everything that would sell. And so liquidation, to Morse, became a matter of trying to turn the place around.

The Lodge's great stone hearth warmed carriage-borne visitors at the midpoint of an excursion around 17-Mile Drive (below, c. 1902).

Morse took over the Hotel Del Monte with the notion that guests should have a good time first and a place to eat and sleep second. He believed strongly in supporting golf and polo as basic to the ambience of the hotel, although at the time they had to be subsidized by the other potentially profit-making units.

The first Hotel Del Monte, which opened in 1880, was a major watering hole for members of high society using the transcontinental railroad net-

Morse threw himself into changing "an old ladies' home" into a first-class resort for the California elite.

work that was either built or acquired by the "Big Four"—Charles Crocker, Collis Potter Huntington, Mark Hopkins and Leland Stanford. To entice more people to ride the train south to San Jose and along the Pacific Coast the Big Four decided to build the hotel on the Monterey Peninsula.

Of this scene Morse later wrote: "Robert Louis Stevenson, who was then living in Monterey, shuddered at the idea of a great caravansary so near his beloved city, and he thought that the place was in for a great change. It occurs to me that if he returned now he would be surprised to learn how much of the Peninsula has been kept intact, with the shoreline for the most part untouched by the sometimes destructive advance of civilization."

The first hotel burned to the ground in the spring of 1887. A second hotel was built on the same site from the same plans and specifications and in the same Victorian Gothic mode as the first, and two wings were added. Between 1908, when Morse first stayed at the hotel, and 1915, when he took over management of P.I., the once exclusive playground for the rich had become what Morse called "something of an old ladies' home." Del Monte Golf Course, built in 1897, was barren of grass fairways and its "greens" were sand; polo had long been abandoned as too expensive; dancing was restricted to one night a week in the art gallery where there wasn't even a bar, and smoking in the main dining room was prohibited. In short, the hotel was drab.

A member of the coming generation, not the passing generation, Morse wanted the hotel to catch up with the times. He redecorated the hotel, revitalized golf, returned polo to the field and restored smoking to the dining room. Dancing, now five nights a week, was moved to the garden lounge, where there was also dining and a bar. The improvements came just in time for the Panama-Pacific International Exposition crowd, down from San Francisco. Business began to pick up immediately.

Morse next turned his attention to golf with the same enthusiasm as he had given to the hotel. When he first saw the Del Monte Golf Course he was almost at a loss for words to describe it :

"There were extraordinary little mounds, called 'chocolate drops,' a type of hazard I had never seen on any other course. They were situated to the right of the first fairway and the bunkers were in a straight line across the fairway. The whole course looked as though it had been laid out with a ruler and there had been no effort to make it conform to the natural contours of the ground."

In order to bring the course to some semblance of playability Morse installed a fairway sprinkler system, replaced the sand "greens" with grass and had all the bunkers redesigned. That was merely the beginning of what would become a legendary golf tradition on the Monterey Peninsula. Most importantly, Morse optimistically began planning a golf course at the old picnic site.

P.I., under Morse's management, seemed in stride with a resurgent nation. Unfortunately, Cornell, not Yale, won the national football champi-

THE BIG FOUR

The Del Monte holdings, to become known as Pebble Beach, began when four Sacramento merchants—*(clockwise from upper left)* Leland Stanford, Charles Crocker, Collis P. Huntington and Mark Hopkins—formed the Central Pacific Railroad Company on June 21, 1861.

Having come from the East Coast during the Gold Rush, Huntington and Hopkins were partners in a hardware store, Stanford owned a grocery store and Crocker was a dry-goods merchant. Of the four, Stanford was the wealthiest by virtue of accepting shares in a mine as payment for an outstanding bill.

In 1868 the Big Four acquired the Southern Pacific Railroad Company, a "paper" company that had plans to build a line from the San Francisco Bay area to Southern California. To encourage passenger traffic south of San Jose they bought the site upon which the Del Monte Hotel was built in 1880.

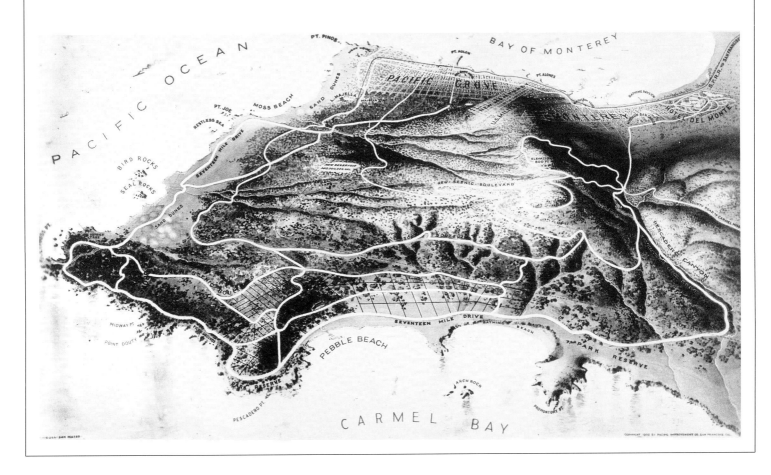

onship in 1915 and J. Pierpont Morgan, who had pulled the country out of a depression slide eight years earlier, was shot by one Erich Muenter.

If the phrase had existed in those days the Del Monte unit would have been pronounced a "turnaround." Morse had certainly accomplished a reversal of losses in less than four years. He was so successful, in fact, that the Del Monte unit was again offered for sale. The asking price was $1.2 million plus inventory and taxes. Through a wealthy friend of Morse's the unit—an estimated 60 percent of the Monterey Peninsula—was offered to a New York syndicate. Incredibly and unarguably the best of the entire scenic area could be purchased in one tidy package but the deal never went through. Such is fate.

The New Yorkers had countered with an offer that was lower than the asking price and the stipulation that Morse continue as manager. Morse, who refused to include himself in the deal, went to the directors of P.I. with the New York bid and a plan of his own. He would buy the Del Monte unit at the asking price he had previously set if he could be given reasonable time to create his own company and secure financing. Morse was certain he would have no trouble getting the loan, which amounted to a total of $1,363,930.70 but he was in for a surprise.

The early Del Monte course was hardy but plain: Sand greens can be seen behind these golfers in 1910.

Two years earlier Morse had become a director of the Crocker National Bank and he had fully expected William H. Crocker, his old mentor, to enter the picture once again. Morse had been a manager under Crocker's guidance and influence for 11 years and Morse obviously placed great personal value on the friendship. But this time Crocker said no. It was time for Morse to go it alone. Many years later Morse remained convinced that a high official within the Crocker National Bank had convinced Crocker that the Del Monte unit would never be profitable.

Shocked and confused but undaunted, Morse went to Herbert Fleishhacker, president of the Anglo Bank in San Francisco. After a site inspection Fleishhacker not only agreed to finance Morse in the acquisition of all the properties within the Del Monte unit but to become a full partner. They purchased the entire package and in return for the land and improvements they took control of all stock, both preferred and common. With that transaction Del Monte Properties Company was formed. It was February 1919 and Morse was 33.

If the New York syndicate couldn't envision what it had passed up, Morse could.

Morse had seen Pebble Beach and imagined a golf links there. He was not the first to do so. In 1913 a proposal for a nine-hole golf course along the cliffs of Pebble Beach was promoted with Carmel guaranteeing a club of 25 players at the rate of $25 per year. A. D. Shepard, a manager of the Pacific

The expanded Hotel Del Monte (left)
burned to the ground in September,
1924, despite the efforts of Billy Parker
(above) and his fire crews. Morse
simply built a third and even larger
Hotel Del Monte.

Early advertisements for Pebble Beach stressed recreation and scenery—and even an electric omnibus to the Lodge!

Improvement Company at the time, moved the plan forward when 25 pledges were made by prospective members. The nine greens were staked out and temporary oil greens were constructed. However, ten prospective members soon backed out (perhaps reacting to the steep price of membership). Shepard still saw the prospect of a full golf links one day, and said that he intended to reserve "all the waterfront down to the course already laid out at the south end." Construction of a golf links on the site had to wait until the end of World War I.

PEBBLE BEACH GOLF LINKS

While the investors' attention was on upgrading the Hotel Del Monte construction of the Pebble Beach Golf Links went forward. Morse wanted to move the California State Amateur championship from Del Monte Golf Course to Pebble Beach. For some two years he played host to many of the leading American and British golfers and listened to their suggestions on how to build a golf course. At least six complete golf course plans were laid out and numerous single holes were planned before Morse made the decision to hire Jack Neville as the designer of the Pebble Beach Golf Links.

At the time Neville was one of Morse's real estate salesmen and he had never designed a golf course although later he participated in several course projects around California. One thing is certain: Jack Neville did know golf.

When he was a child his father owned a home at the Claremont Country Club, set in the hills between Berkeley and Oakland and Neville began playing golf when he was 11. He was in capable hands at Claremont.

The greenskeeper was Jim Smith from Carnoustie, Scotland. Smith had five sons: Willie, Alex, George, Jim and Macdonald. And all five became professionals and made their names in golf. George at the time was the pro at Claremont and Macdonald was his assistant. Willie won the U.S. Open in 1899, and Alex won it twice—first in 1906 and again in 1910 when he defeated his brother Macdonald and Johnny McDermott in a playoff. Add to that list Jim Barnes, winner of the U.S. Open in 1921 and the British Open in 1925. Barnes was assistant greenskeeper at Claremont. As a youngster Neville played golf with these men and took lessons from them after school.

When Morse chose Neville as his designer for Pebble Beach Neville had already won two California State Amateurs and he would go on to win three more and play on the winning 1923 U.S. Walker Cup team. To assist him in bunkering Neville chose Douglas Grant, who had recently returned from six years in the British Isles where he had studied the latest types of bunkering and how greens were made.

In 1921 the tee on the 18th hole was relocated to the promontory on which it sits today. Later, in 1928, H. Chandler Egan lengthened the 18th hole from a 379-yard par 4 to the 548-yard par 5.

When the planning of Pebble Beach began World War I was under way in Europe and the United States would arrive on the European battle front in

Banker Herbert Fleischacker, who financed Morse's plans for Pebble Beach when others turned away.

Jaunty amateur Jack Neville, designer of Pebble Beach Golf Links: "Sam tore up the plans and gave me carte blanche to design the finest championship course possible."

less than two years. At the time golf courses were few and far between on the West Coast and golf course architects did not exist much beyond the Appalachians. It's not surprising then that the men responsible for one of the most challenging and famous golf courses in the world—a course that has baffled professionals as well as weekenders—were all amateur golfers. Grant, also a California Amateur champion, had been a quarterfinalist at the British Amateur; and Egan, who was living at Pebble Beach, was the 1904 and 1905 U.S. Amateur champion.

Neville had first seen the incredible Pebble Beach landscape while playing in—and winning—the 1912 California State Amateur at Del Monte. During a carriage ride along 17-Mile Drive he was so impressed with the scenery that he decided Pebble Beach was where he wanted to live. In 1915, the same year Morse took over P.I., Neville became one of the company's real estate salesman. He was to remain an amateur golfer and real estate salesman under Morse and the future Del Monte Properties Company the rest of his life.

Morse, who loved the game of golf but had little time for it, relied on Neville's recommendations. The one decision Morse did make was to tear up a subdivision plan that Neville had previously drawn. A golf course, not homes, would be built next to the ocean cliffs.

Neville walked the land for three weeks, figuring out how to take advantage of the natural hazards, the beaches, the cliffs and the ocean. As he rightfully saw it, the course should have as many holes along the water as possible. To achieve this he worked out a rough figure-eight design that has gone principally unchanged for more than 70 years. In retrospect that may seem understated but Neville saw the course in a matter-of-fact way.

"It was all there in plain sight," he would explain in later years to golf journalist Herbert Warren Wind. "Very little clearing was necessary. The first three holes moved inland and then back toward the water. The next seven, with the exception of the short fifth, marched along the cliffs. The 11th through 16th looped inland and then back to the water. Then the 17th and the long 18th, which is quite possibly the best finishing hole in golf, edged home along the water."

Neville told Morse what his plans were for the course and nothing was changed. While the landscape of the course flowed naturally—and treacher-

Years later, Morse, himself a onetime cartoonist, and Neville were still celebrated for their prescience.

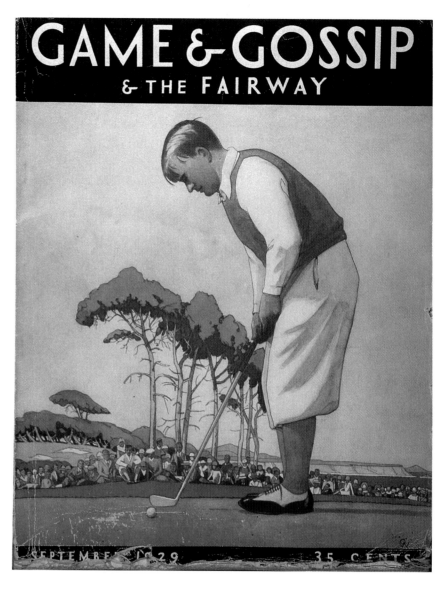

MORSE'S OWN VANITY FAIR

The masthead decreed it "an illustrated journal of social and sporting news and comments," and the description couldn't have been more to the point.

Game & Gossip, the brainstorm of S.F.B. Morse in 1926, was originally a marketing tool to promote interest in the burgeoning Pebble Beach scene. It became a monthly magazine of wit, charm and sophistication, giving insightful coverage of California's social elite. There were columns called "These Charming People," "Frills & Vanities," "Motley Notes of This & That" and "Clothes Line" (the latter, a commentary on fashions). Morse, the former Yale captain, even wrote a piece on football called "Then and Now."

ously—along the terrain, the greens were to become Neville's signature. Neville believed that the golf shots requiring the most skill were the long irons. He felt that a golfer who had the ability to hit a tight target should be rewarded. Small greens were in fashion at the time but Neville made them even smaller.

The year-round condition of the course was also a major concern. Del Monte Golf Course had pioneered the concept of keeping fairways green through all seasons and Pebble Beach was to improve on what Del Monte had started. Neville, not only an outstanding golfer and respected real estate salesman, also published *Pacific Golf and Motor*, the official magazine of the California Automobile Association and the California Golf Association in 1917. In an article discussing the new method for watering the fairways the magazine stated:

"Special sprinklers have been designed that fit right into disappearing connections in the fairways … by grouping divisions of these sprinklers by automatic connections, the necessity for hose is eliminated entirely, and the labor of one man is all that is necessary … "

A total of $22,000 was invested in pipe and another $4,000 for seed. In all,

Working with Jack Neville's links Douglas Grant (left) *brought his ideas about bunkering back from Scotland. Amateur H. Chandler Egan* (right) *made some additional adjustments to the design in the 1920s while preparing the course for the 1929 U.S. Amateur.*

The Nobel Laureate of Cannery Row

Irony has a way of getting to the center of truth and the fact is, John Steinbeck was more at home on the Monterey Peninsula than he was in Salinas, his birthplace.

It was apparent from his early years as a writer that this winner of the Nobel prize for literature was not a popular man in his hometown. Salinas was, after all, a chamber of commerce town, an agribusiness center known as the lettuce capital of the world. *In Dubious Battle* and *The Grapes of Wrath* had alienated Steinbeck from the local burghers.

On the other hand, Monterey had taken him to its breast with the publication of *Cannery Row*, *Tortilla Flat* and *Sweet Thursday*, books that were more romantic in their view than his social criticisms of agriculture and farm-labor life.

Steinbeck was 28 when he settled into a family-owned home in Pacific Grove. That was in 1930 and for most of that decade the Monterey Peninsula—especially the Cannery Row district—was his home away from home.

The Monterey Peninsula, home to such well-known writers as Robert Louis Stevenson, Lincoln Steffens, Mary Austin, Sinclair Lewis, Henry Miller and Robinson Jeffers, was content to let Steinbeck live as a private person. What Steinbeck sought was the companionship of the common people—in some respects the same people he characterized in his novels. Monterey was comfortable with Steinbeck and he was comfortable with Monterey.

When Steinbeck died Dec. 20, 1968 the obituary in the Monterey Peninsula Herald read: "… though he had moved to New York long before his death, he remained a Monterey County boy … "

In 1947 Cannery Row was still the center of the fishing trade and provided Monterey with a significant industry beside tourism. Now the street with a new aquarium is a central attraction for visitors.

total costs for the Pebble Beach Golf Links were estimated at over $100,000. Neville did not charge a fee.

The course would become the ultimate standard against which all other California courses would be compared. Before handicaps were widely established a golfer would compare an unknown golfer's level of ability by asking, "What did you shoot at Pebble Beach?" Holes seven through ten would become known as the most difficult four-hole sequence in golf. The course would test the skills and mettle of amateur and professional and it would glorify or defeat the best. It would become a course that anyone could play for a price but the course never played favorites.

Two holes that remained Neville's favorites were the par-4 eighth and the par-5 18th. "On the eighth," he once said, "you have to play your second shot directly over a cliff and it must carry 180 yards or it's in the ocean. You can go around the cliff but it costs you an extra shot.

"On the 18th, the worst thing you can do is hook, because it's ocean all down the left side. The fairway gets narrower as you approach the green. The opening on the front side is only about five feet, with sand traps right in front. The small opening makes it tough to get there in two. I was able to get pin high there a couple of times, but I've never been on the green in two."

Neville, destined for golf immortality as the designer of Pebble Beach, was a self-effacing man. The completion of the Pebble Beach Golf Links brought a sophisticated order to Morse's plans. Simultaneously, a reconstructed lodge (the original burned the day after Christmas, 1917) was added to a row of cottages that had recently been built overlooking Stillwater Cove and the golf course. The golf course and lodge opened the same month that Morse formed his new company: February, 1919. Pebble Beach was on its way to becoming the most famous golf resort in existence.

The days of the Hotel Del Monte had set the social tone. Princes, dukes, maharajahs, even an aging General William Sherman and a young Howard Hughes, Salvador Dali, Charles Lindbergh, Harry Vardon and others Morse called "the glitter and the pomp," had been guests at the great hotel during an era that spanned more than half a century. Pebble Beach had arrived early on and that was just the beginning.

Predictably, Pebble Beach Golf Links became golf's mecca and players of all abilities and all walks of life came from all corners of the globe to challenge its caliber. If the old Hotel Del Monte was the passing of an era Pebble Beach was the beginning of a new elegance.

Still to come was the survival of 13 years of Prohibition, the burning of the Hotel Del Monte in 1924 and its reconstruction two years later, the opening of the Monterey Peninsula Country Club in 1926 and the Cypress Point Club in 1928, the Great Depression, the Del Monte Golf Course land purchase in 1937, the World War II "duration," the $2.2 million sale of the Hotel Del Monte to the Navy in 1948, the opening of Spyglass Hill Golf Course in 1966 and The Links at Spanish Bay in 1987.

From 1919 forward Pebble Beach has exuded the flavor of the classic

European spa; an atmosphere of wealth and exclusivity that attracted nobility, presidents, celebrities, artists, musicians, athletes, industrialists and statesmen. In 1928 it was Prince George doing his version of the "Varsity Drag." In 1941 it was Ginger Rogers at a picnic. In 1947 it was Bing Crosby mixing with the gallery at his first pro-am tournament. In 1956 it was President Dwight D. Eisenhower playing a round at Cypress. In 1960 it was John F. Kennedy, a senator then, posing on the lawn in front of the Lodge. In 1966 it was an incognito Beatle Ringo Starr golfing and riding horseback through Del Monte Forest. In 1989 it was Huey Lewis playing impromptu harmonica on the golf course at the AT&T Pebble Beach National Pro-Am. In 1991 it was Pavarotti singing everything from "Otello" to "O Sole Mio" in a tent at a fundraising concert.

The aura of Pebble Beach was to capture everyone's imagination. To play golf or privately retreat in a beautiful setting may have been reason enough to visit Pebble Beach but Hollywood had its own vision. Countless movies have been made at Pebble Beach, including "Follow The Sun," the story of Ben Hogan starring Glenn Ford and Anne Baxter. Pebble Beach was the natural setting for the 1950 Hogan film. The great golfer, sometimes known as

In 1960, Morse & Co. broke ground for the shore course of the Monterey Peninsula Country Club (p. 186).

the "grim genius," had won the 1949 Crosby at Pebble Beach before miraculously surviving an auto accident that same year.

But the most arresting movie ever shot at Pebble Beach was "National Velvet," filmed on location in 1944 and starring Elizabeth Taylor and Mickey Rooney.

If Morse wanted to give notability to Pebble Beach by moving the California Amateur from Del Monte he was more than successful. Pebble Beach's reputation as an outstanding golf course was to reach the East just before the Depression was to shroud the nation. Fortunately, arrangements were made in time for Pebble Beach to host the 1929 U.S. Amateur Championship. Until then it had gained regional stature but at the U.S. Men's Amateur the course made its nationwide debut.

The U.S. Women's Amateur followed in 1940, and after World War II both tournaments returned to Pebble Beach: the U.S. Amateur in 1947 and 1961, and the U.S. Women's Amateur in 1948. The course would go on to host a PGA Championship in 1977 and three U.S. Open Championships (1972, 1982 and 1992), but an informal gathering of golfing buddies called the Bing Crosby National Pro-Am, also known as "The Clambake" for the party that

Like other men of accomplishment Morse found relaxation in learning new skills, including painting.

THE FABULOUS FOLK WHO CAME TO PLAY

Through the years, Pebble Beach became a destination for the famous and powerful, the admired and the scandalous. Clockwise from left: Bette Davis making the Pacific look good; Morse and Ginger Rogers in her salad days; Salvador Dali and friend kidnapping monarchs; Sinclair Lewis in a rare moment of serenity.

Clockwise from right: Charles Lindbergh posed with his plane near the links; Gerald Ford hosted the 1982 U.S. Open; Senator John F. Kennedy just before winning the nomination for President; Erroll Flynn takes a breather; Ringo Starr rides the day after the Beatles' last scheduled public concert, in August 1966.

accompanied the tournament, placed Pebble Beach before the masses.

In 1947 Bing Crosby moved the tournament from Rancho Santa Fe in southern California to Pebble Beach. Crosby had pioneered the perfect match between professional golfers and amateurs by adding celebrities to the lineup and giving the proceeds to charity. The tournament has since expanded from 54 holes to 72.

When national television began its coverage of the Crosby tournament in 1958 millions of golfers and lovers of natural beauty could view Pebble Beach from their living rooms. Technology had taken the golf course far beyond Morse's earliest dreams.

Pebble Beach Golf Links, founded by a visionary, designed by amateurs and challenged by the best golfers the world could offer, fulfilled its founder's vision—of a destination that would be sought after and would furnish some of the game's great moments.

Morse died on May 10, 1969. He was 83.

Glenn Ford as Ben Hogan eyes a drive at Pebble Beach Golf Links in the hit film "Follow the Sun."

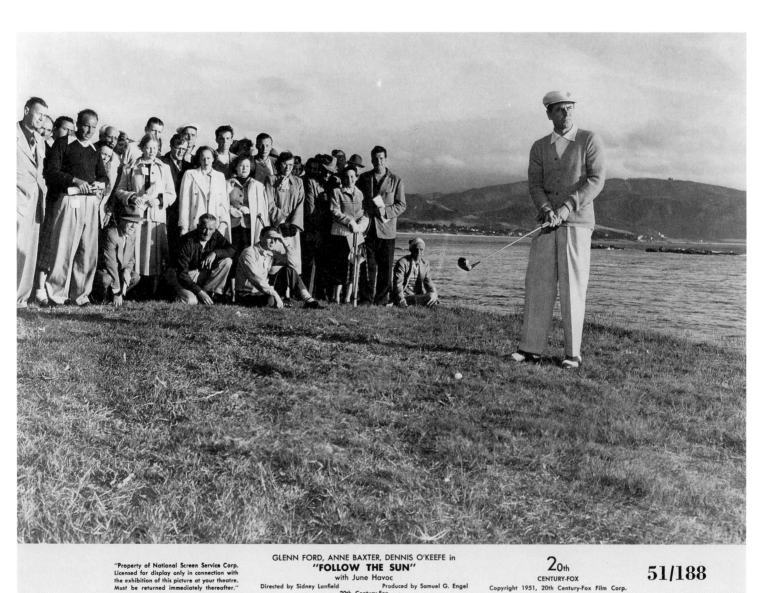

GLENN FORD, ANNE BAXTER, DENNIS O'KEEFE in
"FOLLOW THE SUN"
with June Havoc
Directed by Sidney Lanfield   Produced by Samuel G. Engel
20th Century-Fox

20th
CENTURY-FOX
Copyright 1951, 20th Century-Fox Film Corp.

51/188

The real-life love story of Valerie and Ben Hogan —Two kids from Texas!

FOLLOW THE SUN

GLENN **FORD** · ANNE **BAXTER** · DENNIS **O'KEEFE**

JUNE HAVOC

LARRY KEATING · ROLAND WINTERS · NANA BRYANT

SCREEN PLAY BY FREDERICK HAZLITT BRENNAN

PRODUCED BY
SAMUEL G. ENGEL

20th CENTURY-FOX

DIRECTED BY
SIDNEY LANFIELD

BASED ON AN ARTICLE BY FREDERICK HAZLITT BRENNAN · PUBLISHED IN THE READER'S DIGEST

No matter how hard it tried Hollywood couldn't make its movie larger than Ben Hogan himself.

In the 1982 U.S. Open Tom Watson (above) made a miracle recovery to beat Jack Nicklaus, who a decade earlier had won his own U. S. Open at Pebble Beach (right).

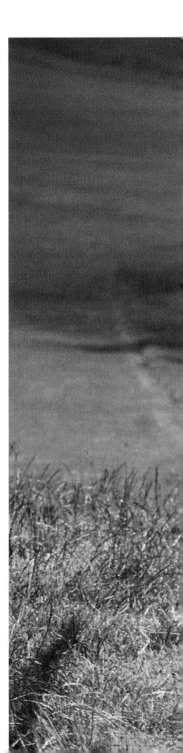

The Best and Brightest

If ever a golf resort were to spawn outrageous stories and verifiable feats of athletic heroism on the course, it would be Pebble Beach. Certainly modern history can easily recount Tom Watson's astonishing victory at the 1982 U.S. Open, or Jack Nicklaus' rarest of doubles, winning the U.S. Amateur and U.S. Open at the same site. On the following pages are some of Pebble Beach's greatest moments as they were recorded in memory, in print and on film.

"We Pledge Ourselves by Our Faith in the Cherry Tree to Turn in Honest Score Cards"

R. R. Flint of Sacramento administering the "golfers' oath" at the cherry tree planted at Del Monte in honor of George Washington, as the feature of the celebration held at the resort last Saturday. Left to right—J. W. Byrne, Harold Sampson, Vincent Whitney, C. Burman, George Turnbull, R. R. Flint, Clifford Weatherwax and Douglas Grant.

U-Boat Damages Hull of Motorship At Los Angeles

NEW LODGE AT DEL MONTE OPENED BY JOYOUS THRONG

DEL MONTE, February 23.—A Messrs. George Montgomery, Jessie

flowers applied to skirt. Mrs. Vincent Whitney—Rose velvet and tulle, slippers and stockings to match. Mrs. Comyn—Black silk net. Miss Corbel—Black tulle and spangles. Mrs. Horace Hill—Black Spanish lace gown. Mrs. Felton Elkins—Colonial gown of white net and pale blue. Mrs. Roger Bocqueraz—White silk and pearls. Mrs. W. H. Poole—Gown of black satin trimmed with silver

conventional flowers for trimming. Mrs. Cyril Tobin—Black satin quite long and draped, green fan. Miss Emelie Tubbs—Velvet in an odd shape of pink. Miss Marie Louise Winslow—Pink silk, draped gown. Miss Lucy Hanchett—Midnight blue satin. Miss Dorothy Crawford—Dark blue velvet. Mrs. Isaac Upham—Black gown of jet paillettes with diamonds

The San Francisco press preserved the moment Pebble Beach Golf Links opened with a promise and a laugh.

THE GRAND OPENING—1919

It was 1919 and 33-year-old S.F.B. Morse was throwing a party for history to appreciate—the grand opening of the Lodge and its accompanying Pebble Beach Golf Links.

There had been some rain, but the timing seemed perfect for the opening of the Lodge and its new golf course along the bluffs of Carmel Bay. The Western Front had fallen thankfully silent just months earlier, President Woodrow Wilson had embarked for Europe with his ill-destined 14 points for "peace without victory," Henry Ford's Model T was an assembly-line success and Prohibition was still a year away.

The country was anxiously returning to "normalcy." It was an excellent time for reviving a socially composed way of enjoying life and its luxuries.

For days before the Washington's Birthday weekend, the society pages of San Francisco's competing dailies were full of superlatives describing who was already there, who was coming, what they were doing and what they were wearing when they did it.

A cherry tree would be planted in front of The Lodge, a golf tournament played, polo matches held between a Del Monte team and visiting Burlingame and, of course, a grand dinner would encompass the entire Lodge.

"The new Lodge has been the source of no end of favorable comment. It has been constructed with all the modern comforts and conveniences of a metropolitan hotel ... ," gushed *The American* in its Saturday evening edition. The cherry tree was planted by Edward Simpson, the young son of a prominent Tacoma family, in honor of George Washington, according to an account by one Lady Teazle. Mr. R.R. Flint of Sacramento administered the golfers' oath: "We pledge ourselves by our faith in the cherry tree to turn in honest scorecards."

Fizz, 1-Up

A story Morse savored took place at Del Monte during the finals of the California State Amateur. As Morse told it, here's what happened:

"In the early days of the state championship, the event was a great deal of fun. Everybody who took part stayed in the old Hotel Del Monte and there were only about 60 to 80 players up until the time it came to Pebble Beach. With few exceptions the players were all friends and they brought with them their families and more friends, and the event was a Gala!

"I think one of the most amusing stories happened one of the years that Scotty Armstrong, who by the way everybody loved, won the championship, which he did several times. (Scotty Armstrong was Ervin S. Armstrong, a scratch player from Midwick Country Club in Los Angeles. Known as the "greatest fighter of them all," he had won the California Amateur Championship in 1911 and 1915 when this story unfolded).

"Prohibition was in the offing and there was a lot of talk about it. The tournament went down to the finals and Scotty was opposed by Heine Schmidt. Scotty was a *bon vivant* and a happy-go-lucky individual who enjoyed life to the fullest. Heine was a total abstainer and he took his golf—and everything else—very seriously.

"The event was just before the First World War. I think it was perhaps the first year that Peter Hay went to work for us. Anyway, he was presiding in the matter of starting off the players. On the day of the finals there was a good gallery—in those days that meant a few hundred people at the most. No gallery was expected to go 18 holes without a drink, and for that matter, most of the players felt in need

Bobby Jones returned years after the 1929 U. S. Amateur to talk golf with Pebble Beach's Peter Hay.

CALIFORNIA

of something at about the ninth hole. So, we had a gay pavilion at the ninth hole where drinks were dispensed to the needy.

"Everybody waited anxiously for Scotty to show up. Heine had been on the putting green for an hour before he was slated to play. He was getting more and more anxious. Finally, it got to be 20 minutes after starting time and Peter, with his Scotch burr, announced that he was afraid he would have to award the championship to Heine by default. Just as he was about to do so, Scotty showed up—in his dinner coat! He hadn't been to bed!!

"He yelled out to wait a few minutes and he rushed into the caddie

THIRTY THIRD
**National Amateur
Golf Championship**
PEBBLE BEACH
CALIFORNIA
1929

DEL MONTE

The 1929 U.S. Amateur had a program with a specially commisioned painting on its cover.

house where he took off his dinner jacket, put a belt around his dinner trousers, put on his golf shoes, rolled up his sleeves, had a gin fizz, and appeared on the first tee.

"They both played brilliant golf. They reached the ninth hole and Scotty felt very much in need of another gin fizz. Heine could hardly contain his annoyance, but he had to wait, to be a good sportsman.

"To make a long story short, Scotty won on the 18th hole and as I walked out to greet him and congratulate him, he said, with a wide grin, 'The wets win!' "

BOBBY'S PREMONITION

The U.S. Men's Amateur went west for the first time in 1929, and with it came all expectations that the great Robert Tyre (Bobby) Jones, Jr. would be the eventual winner. Fate had other plans for Jones that year.

After his practice rounds and, after finishing as medalist, Jones would sip a bourbon and visit with Morse. One evening before match play began, Jones confided to Morse that he had always been apprehensive of an 18-hole match. He felt that at 36 holes the best golfer would win most of the time, but at 18 holes a lesser player could start out with two birdies and be difficult to catch.

That's precisely what happened when he met little-known Johnny Goodman in the first round of match play in the 1929 U.S. Amateur at Pebble Beach. Goodman jumped into the lead with two birdies and Jones was never to take the lead. After the match, Jones told Morse that in the future when he was playing an 18-hole match he would mentally start two holes down. (The trick must have worked–the next year Jones achieved his never-equalled "Grand Slam" series of victories.)

Obscure Johnny Goodman surprised Bob Jones (below) in 1929, a time when galleries could get close.

TARGET GOLF

During a practice round at Del Monte before the 1929 U.S. Men's Amateur began a film crew was shooting Bobby Jones in action.

"Shoot for that fellow in the tree," the director instructed Jones, pointing to the cameraman about 150 yards down the first fairway.

"Shoot right for him?" Jones asked.

"Don't worry, you won't hit him. Besides we want to have the ball coming toward the camera," the director told Jones.

Jones teed off, hitting the camera and nearly killing the man in the tree.

CONSOLATION WINNER

Not all great moments in golf take place in tournament play. For Mary Morse, S.F.B. Morse's daughter, it came after she lost in the quarterfinal of the 1940 U.S. Women's Amateur at Pebble Beach.

At 13, Mary had been women's champion at the Monterey Peninsula Country Club, so area golfers weren't surprised when she qualified with an 85, just one stroke back of Betty Jameson who would go on to successfully

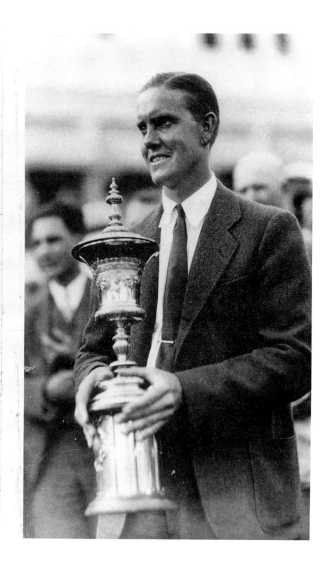

Betty Jameson (above) *was undaunted by hard hazards in the 1940 U.S. Women's Amateur. Harrison R. Johnston* (left) *in 1929 became one of only two golfers to interrupt Bob Jones' string of five Amateur Championships.*

Two Amateur Champions of the '40s: Betty Jameson with trophy, 1940; Skee Riegel getting out of trouble, 1947.

defend her title. Mary and Clara Callender, who had played on the Pacific Grove High School team, were the only local women out of 163 entries. Morse eventually lost to Marjorie Ferrir, who was pushed to a course record in the process.

After the loss, Patty Berg, the former U.S. Amateur champion who had just turned pro and would go into the annals of golf as one of the all-time greats, walked up to Mary and asked if she wanted to play a round.

"She just said, 'Let's play'," Mary recalled. "And we did. We had a big gallery, too."

Some consolation round.

ALWAYS THE SPORTSMAN

Bobby Jones returned to Pebble Beach in 1947, this time as a spectator at the 1947 U.S. Men's Amateur. At this point in his career, almost twenty

years after his retirement from competitive golf, Jones was still regarded as a golfing hero, and his opinion about a competition was eagerly sought. Asked who he thought would win, Jones looked over the field of 210 entries which included defending champion Stanley Bishop, former winner Harrison "Jimmie" Johnston, Dick Chapman and Marvin Ward, all past U.S. Amateur champs. He picked his old 1929 nemesis Johnny Goodman. Goodman went out in the fourth round.

ALL THE FASHION

Robert H. "Skee" Riegel won the 1947 U.S. Amateur at Pebble and instantly became a favorite of the press. Golf writers, always looking for "color," found him good copy. "Skee," one writer reported, "wears the loudest socks on the course, crams his cap over one ear like an Apache, and smokes cigarettes down so close you can almost hear his lips sizzle."

CONTINENTAL CHAMPION

The 1948 U.S. Women's Amateur Championship featured players aiming for their first American national title, and there was some liklihood of a new name emerging: only two former champions were competing, with familiar names such as Patty Berg, Babe Zaharias, and Betty Jameson having

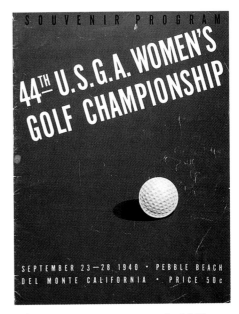

Above, an austere program in 1940. Below left, Skee Riegel on his way to winning the U.S. Men's Amateur Championship in 1947.

just turned professional. Played at Pebble Beach for the second time, the U.S. Women's Amateur left some sportswriters unimpressed. (Charles Bartlett of the Chicago Tribune wrote "the [final] match was undistinguished by good golf.") However, Grace Lenczyk of Newington, Connecticut, did distinguish herself geographically. Lenczyk had been brought into golf ten years earlier by two brothers who caddied at a golf club near their home. She'd developed a powerful swing, and the papers referred to her as "stolid [and] strongly built." Having already won the Canadian Women's Amateur, Lenczyk celebrated the week of her 21st birthday by ripping through the competition, finally defeating runnerup Helen Sigel 4 and 3, to become, as one wag put it, "the amateur champion of everything from the North Pole to the Mexican border."

SAFE ON SECOND

Some great moments in golf come from a player's advance planning rather than his miraculous performance on the course. Jack Nicklaus' play in the 1961 U.S. Amateur is a perfect example of this.

The 21-year-old Nicklaus was keenly aware that he could get in serious trouble at the second hole if he ignored its hidden dangers. At 497 yards, this straightaway par-5 looks relatively easy from a scratch golfer's point of

This routine—and planned—sand save on No. 2 helped Jack Nicklaus win the 1961 U. S. Amateur.

view, but Nicklaus knew he had to keep his drive to the right side if he was going to be successful. Anything to the left raised the demand on a second shot, not because of the bunkering, which was not threatening to Nicklaus, but because of branches and rough left and back of the green.

His tee shot dictated whether he would play an offensive or defensive iron to the green. In fact, Nicklaus' second shot went into the left greenside bunker, and he made a routine shot out. Because he planned ahead of time he never encountered any problems with the second hole as he went on to win his second U.S. Amateur Championship. Later he wrote, "I like the second at Pebble very much, perhaps because it looks like such a pushover but can destroy you unless you handle it with care ... I have never since handled Pebble Beach this capably, never had as many accurate, full-blooded long irons to those small greens, never made so few erratic shots."

When Nicklaus completed his win (8 and 6 over Dudley Wysong) he was 20 strokes under par for the 112 holes he had played in eight matches.

"BLOCKING" WILL DO IT EVERY TIME

Jack Nicklaus had history on his mind in 1972. He had won the PGA the year before and the Masters two months earlier, and he knew going in that winning the U.S. Open at Pebble Beach would bring him to within one of

Jack Nicklaus, at 21, displays the symbols of his second U. S. Amateur, won on his favorite course.

Bobby Jones' major win records.

So, when he approached the next to the last hole of the tournament—the storybook 17th—it was understandable if he was a little tight in the elbow; he had, after all, taken a six on No. 10. Fortunately for history and his game, Nicklaus had his tempo and his confidence when he hit a 1-iron toward the green. The ball ripped through the headwind, hit the pin and dropped just two inches from the hole.

It was called one of the great finishing shots in golf as Nicklaus went on to defeat Bruce Crampton by three shots, 290 to 293 over 72 holes, but Nicklaus candidly admitted that it wasn't the shot he had in mind.

"I got the clubface a little closed and the club a little too far to the inside too quickly," Nicklaus said later. "Normally such errors early in the swing will wreck the shot. This time, having such great tempo, I was able to adjust by 'blocking' just a fraction through impact. The result was a low, drilling-type shot that bored straight through the wind, hit the pin and nearly went into the hole."

Back in the pack was Tom Watson, 15 strokes behind Nicklaus and 10 years before his time.

Pebble Beach has been kind to Jack Nicklaus, even if he was denied the U.S. Open in '82, and Nicklaus has been kind to Pebble Beach.

Jack Nicklaus wins the 1972 U.S. Open, his second national title at Pebble Beach Golf Links.

Lanny Wadkins takes to the air as the putt drops that clinches his first major title, the 1977 PGA Championship.

In winning the 1961 U.S. Amateur and the 1972 U.S. Open, both at Pebble Beach, he became the only man to win those championships on the same course. Add to those major wins his three Bing Crosby National Pro-Am titles (1967, 1972 and 1973) and it's understandable why Nicklaus feels the way he does about Pebble.

"If I had only one round of golf to play, I would choose to play it at Pebble Beach," Nicklaus once wrote.

I TAKE THAT BACK

After the third round of the 1977 PGA Championship, Lanny Wadkins said to Gene Littler that he hoped Littler would win the tournament. At the time "Gene the Machine" was six strokes ahead of Wadkins with only 18 holes to play the next day.

But in the final round Littler soared to a 76 and Wadkins, who had been playing steady par or better golf each day, came in with a 70. Now facing a sudden-death playoff, Wadkins changed his mind about whom he wanted to win. The two started at the first and played even for two holes and then Wadkins made a six-foot par putt on the par-4 3rd at Pebble Beach, clinching the PGA title.

THE WILY WATSON

Tom Watson knows that Nicklaus is not the only great golfer to find luck and fame at Pebble Beach's 17th.

It was the 1982 U.S. Open, and Watson stood at the tee of the 71st hole, the par-3 17th with its roller-coaster green surrounded by forest-high rough, bunkers all around and ocean on the left. Nicklaus was in at 284, and all he could do was wait.

Watson had misplayed the 16th, scoring a bogey and falling back into a tie with Nicklaus. He had just two holes to recover and his chances dimmed when his tee shot landed in the rough behind the green.

"I'm going to make it," he told his caddie, who had advised him to play it safe. The rest is Pebble Beach history. Make the shot, he did. Watson went into a jubilant war dance and then finished with another birdie to win by two.

Fun at the Crosby: Dean Martin and Phil Harris, pro Peter Hay with Jack Benny, Bob Hope in a new cap. Bing fights an uphill battle on Pebble Beach's eighth (left) and Ben Hogan goes on radio (above).

At Something Called "The Clambake"

Nothing brought more fame or recognition to Pebble Beach than Bing Crosby's golf tournament. Relocated to the Monterey Peninsula in 1947 after six years at Rancho Santa Fe, the Crosby, as everyone called it, became an American institution. It mixed the leading pros with show-business celebrities, politicians, businessmen and the top amateurs for a week of golf and laughter. The weather was often bad and occasionally atrocious, as in 1962 when an overnight snowfall postponed the fourth round. The intial purse was $10,000; in 1992 it was $1,100,000. The original venues were Pebble Beach, Cypress Point and the Monterey Peninsula Country Club. Spyglass Hill replaced the MPCC in 1967 and Poppy Hills supplanted Cypress Point in 1991. Crosby played until 1957, and in 1958 he became the tournament's television analyst.

The stars of show business entertained the tour pros, golf writers and other guests at the Clambake party. Obviously enjoying the show are a happy Ben Hogan (left) *and Cary Middlecoff and Jack Burke, Jr.* (right).

Bing Crosby is honored by a plaque near the first tee at Pebble Beach.

The Crosby was tailored perfectly for television, with its blend of scenic courses, top pros, celebrities and a captive winter audience in large portions of the country. A major part of its enormous appeal was the presence of the celebrities: Bob Hope, Dean Martin, Phil Harris, Jack Lemmon, Clint Eastwood, James Garner, Andy Williams, Robert Stack and, in later years, new stars like movie zany Bill Murray and whoever happens to be quarterbacking the San Francisco 49ers. Harris played for 25 years, winning the pro-am with Dutch Harrison in 1951 by sinking a putt estimated to be 90 feet on 17. Today the Crosby lives on in the colors of the AT&T Pebble Beach National Pro-Am.

Sharing a moment of relaxation at the clinic preceding the tournament, Phil Harris, James Garner and Arnold Palmer (above) make like the Three Musketeers. Pro Cam Puget, Crosby and Samuel F.B. Morse, the founder of Pebble Beach, at a long-ago Crosby (left) and, on the facing page, Bing as so many of his legion of golfing buddies remember him.

It's A Lot More Than Just Golf

Tradition is what fuels events at Pebble Beach. Over 100 years ago high society from San Francisco and the East Coast came by passenger train to stay at the Hotel Del Monte. With the beautiful Monterey Peninsula as a backdrop there were endless rounds of refined golf, the excitement of high-goal polo, the thrill of the hunt, the self-satisfaction of showing a pedigreed dog and, of course, more golf.

When the era of the Hotel Del Monte came to a close and a new future began at Pebble Beach the tradition of hosting important events followed. Traced back to the turn of the century it is this heritage that continues today. The atmosphere is the same now as it was back then; the only difference today is that a greater spectrum of people come to Pebble Beach for an even greater—and unforgettable—experience.

Golf remains the unchallenged main attraction at Pebble Beach but for thousands of visitors each year—golfers included—Pebble Beach also means classic cars, blue-ribbon dogs, Olympic-caliber equines, world-class regattas and notable wine tastings. Over the years these special events have become as much a tradition at Pebble Beach as golf. Well, almost.

There's a world of recreation in Monterey and some of it is pretty high-flying.

Samuel F. B. Morse felt that polo would be as alluring as golf in bringing guests to Monterey. Although golf now reigns supreme polo competition still drew crowds at Collins Field until recently.

For decades lovers of equestrian sports have come to a nearly hidden spot near the golf courses to pursue the precise art of jumping rails and more natural obstacles as well.

EQUESTRIAN SPORT AND SHOW

Just inland, in the privacy of the pines above The Lodge, is the Pebble Beach Equestrian Center. This is where Olympic hopefuls come to train and compete in dressage and cross-country, where the finest horse trainers and showers of the West Coast congregate each August for the annual Pebble Beach Summer Horse and Dressage Shows.

It's at the Pebble Beach Equestrian Center's Collins Field that the tradition of polo which began at the Hotel Del Monte was revitalized each season until 1990 in playing the California Challenge Match, a spirited competition between the best high-goal players of northern and southern California.

The breeders' and trainers' proud pupils play up to the judges but remain a kid's best friend.

A CLASSIC CANINE CONVOCATION

"Pebble Beach" to the owner or handler of a champion dog means the Classic of the Pacific, staged by the Del Monte Kennel Club. One of the oldest and most respected events of its kind, the show dates back to its beginnings at the Hotel Del Monte.

Virtually in a class of its own, the Classic of the Pacific has rigorous acceptance standards and accepts only 500 dogs, all of which must be previous blue-ribbon winners. This limitation distinguishes the Classic of the Pacific from other dog shows which may allow three times as many entries. In its exclusivity, the Classic of the Pacific is thus much like the Pebble Beach *Concours d'Elegance* or the AT&T Pebble Beach National Pro-Am.

In the realm of pedigreed dogs, there is nothing like witnessing champions going through their routines for the judges at Pebble Beach. Perhaps it's because of the show's spectacular site. In tribute to the incomparable beauty of the setting the Classic of the Pacific—like the Pebble Beach *Concours d'Elegance*—is held overlooking Pebble Beach's 18th green.

The Classic of the Pacific reaches its climax at—where else?—the lawn that spreads out below the Lodge.

For excitement and a good view of the Monterey Peninsula and surrounding countryside, try the daring sport of hot air ballooning.

MONTEREY COUNTY'S HOT AIR AFFAIR

For an all-out adrenaline draw, hot air ballooning has to be it. There is nothing on earth like the sensation of ascending on the early-morning thermals. The views of Monterey Peninsula, the mountains to the south and the Pacific Ocean are breathtaking, and the quiet, interrupted from time to time by the roar of a hot-air engine, is unmatched.

In late February each year the annual Monterey County Hot Air Affair attracts the country's best balloonists who compete in what they call the "hare and the hound" event. If you're over five years of age and want to experience a tamer version of the sport there are tethered balloon rides.

DIZZY, CHICK, AND ALL THAT JAZZ

The Monterey Jazz Festival, like other Peninsula happenings, is the oldest continually running event of its kind in the United States. It keeps going because, as trumpeter Dizzy Gillespie observed, "Monterey's like home. Monterey's the best."

The Monterey Jazz Festival, held each September, was founded in 1958 and has been staged in the Monterey County Fairgrounds area every year since. That first year the lineup included Dizzy Gillespie, Mel Lewis, MJQ, Billie Holiday, Ernestine Anderson, Dave Brubeck, Max Roach and Harry James. And in 34 years, there has been no letup. In more recent years, there have been the Count Basie Orchestra, Jon Hendricks & Company, Shorty Rogers/Bud Shank and The Lighthouse All Stars, Chick Corea Akoustic Band and Diane Schuur, to name a few. One year, local jazz pianist Jan Deneau, doing an Erroll Garner retrospective, received a standing ovation. The fans come because they love the music and also because the music loves the casual outdoor atmosphere of Monterey's fairgrounds.

Some of the world's most celebrated chefs at the Masters of Food and Wine event. Above left, Julia Child takes a bow while Paul Bocuse, left, livens up a flambé and Chef Nobu Matsuhisa displays his cutting edge.

A Celebration of Table and Vine

Following the European tradition of honoring new wine—and announcing its worthiness—hundreds of wine aficionados gather at the Inn at Spanish Bay each year on the third Thursday in November to sip and judge the newly arrived Beaujolais Nouveau.

In late February and early March, the Masters of Food and Wine brings together the finest international roster of chefs and wine makers to be assembled anywhere. The atmosphere is intimate and heady. Marcella Hazan, Paul Bocuse, Mumm's Steven Brauer, Karl Josef Fuchs, Bradley Ogden, Peter Gorges, Charles Palmer, Patrick Clark, Gerhard Michler and Nobu Matsuhisa were the headliners at just one recent Masters of Food and Wine gathering at the Highland Inn.

Wine and food events bring chefs and wine lovers from all parts of the world to sample Monterey's hospitality.

Catamarans, dories and every sail craft imaginable dance on the waves of the Pacific near the Monterey Peninsula. In the summertime, regatta competition on racecourses (below) is at its peak.

A Meeting of Wind and Waves

Flanked by the bluffs bordering the fourth and sixth fairways of Pebble Beach Golf Links is serene Stillwater Cove with its "island" outcropping in the center. Beginning in May and continuing into September, a series of regattas are launched from this protected body of water. From the distant shoreline there is a near-mystic aura over Carmel Bay as the sailboats, gliding through the race-course, move quietly in and out of offshore fogbanks. Races such as the Labor Day Mercury Invitational, Stuart Haldorn Regatta and the S.F.B. Morse Regatta are fixtures at Pebble Beach and favorites among spectators.

THE SPORTING LIFE ON MONTEREY BAY

One of the richest and most diverse ocean resources in the world is Monterey Bay, recently named the nation's largest marine sanctuary, which is best understood as being comparable to a huge underwater national forest. The bay, 20 miles across at its farthest point, is bisected by a submarine canyon, more than a mile deep and as steep and wide as the Grand Canyon. The subterranean inhabitants range from minute jellyfish to plumed anemones four feet high. Sea otters, sea lions and seals are year-round tenants. Visitors are blue, hump-backed and orca whales. The gray whales move in for the winter. Kelp forests, deep reefs and sandy seabottoms form the floor of the bay. Commercial and sports fishermen co-exist harmoniously, while water sports include kayaking near the coast and scuba diving. Occasionally you might have the opportunity to swim with a dolphin. The view is great from Point Pinos, where the bay joins the Pacific Ocean. If you want to see more marine life and stay dry, visit the Monterey Bay Aquarium.

The waters of Monterey Bay offer a wide range of diversions, from playful seals and kayaking (left) *to scuba diving* (below).

The Monarch butterfly, a popular winter visitor, is a protected species during migration.

HONORING THE MONARCH

The Monterey Peninsula also has its "own" events. These are special times that mean more to the residents than to visitors but for an insider's view of locals at play they shouldn't be missed. Every hometown has its own special character and Pacific Grove, which proudly calls itself "the last hometown," is no different. One of the Peninsula's autumn highlights since 1939 has been the children's "Butterfly Parade" held each October in Pacific Grove. The engaging march honors the Monarch butterfly, a winter resident of Pacific Grove.

Small children hold center stage as Pacific Grove welcomes back the butterflies with an October parade.

Indy race cars and motorcycles provide the action at Laguna Seca, under the auspices of the Sports Car Racing Association of the Monterey Peninsula.

In Search of Speed at Laguna Seca

Auto and motorcycle racing buffs gather four times each year at Laguna Seca, one of the top tracks in the country. The Peninsula air vibrates with the roar of the high-tech engines powering Indy race cars and high-speed motorcycles. Each of the four races lasts three days, with plenty of action on the track and in the pits. The track opened in 1957 when the races moved from the narrow tree-lined roads of Del Monte Forest. There was just one race on the calendar at that time. Now the competitions draw some 350,000 spectators annually. Several thousand volunteers contribute their time and effort to the racing events that have raised more than $5 million for area charities. One of the features of the season is the annual historic auto race which has for 19 years attracted entires from throughout the world. It is held in conjunction with the Pebble Beach *Concours d'Elegance*, the car show supreme. For more on the *Concours* at Pebble Beach, turn to the next page.

THE CRÈME DE LA CRÈME OF CLASSIC CARS

Mention Pebble Beach to a classic car enthusiast and the image of exquisite beauty, unparalleled challenge and unique status is automatic. But instead of golf the image is of the Pebble Beach *Concours d'Elegance*.

To car collectors the world over the spectacularly regal event is the most significant of its kind; an invitation to exhibit is akin to an amateur's playing in the AT&T Pebble Beach National Pro-Am or a pro qualifying for the U.S. Open Championship.

This is the *concours* where Jay Leno wanders through and no one looks up, where Clint Eastwood says hello to old friends, where Bob Hope made

(continued)

On facing page, elegance gains new meaning in the back seat of a classic car. Left, Ralph Lauren shows his Best-of-Show Bugatti Atlantic. Across bottom, the symbols of greatness.

an unannounced and hilariously impromptu appearance on the ramp and where San Francisco columnist Herb Caen once handed out trophies and quips to the winners. Pebble Beach is the *concours* to which Lucius Beebe, newspaperman, columnist and *bon vivant* back in the late 1950s, rode the train. His very own train, of course.

The Pebble Beach *Concours d'Elegance* is the anchor event of a summer automotive weekend that has been compared only with Monaco. One Saturday and Sunday each August the Monterey Peninsula is transformed into a world of expensive and exotic cars and the people they attract. By day, cars valued in the millions line up at Pebble Beach for judging while at Laguna Seca Raceway the classic race cars of yesterday speed around the track. By night, cars are sold to the highest bidders at glittering auctions.

No other *concours* in the world can match that.

The Pebble Beach *Concours d'Elegance* has been the epitome of what all other events hope to be: the consummate classic car show. Each year, while its imitators try to catch up, the Pebble Beach version tops what it had accomplished the year before.

In 1985, an exceptional year even for Pebble Beach, the only six Bugatti Royales ever made were brought together for the first time. In total there were 30 Bugattis of varying types on the manicured lawn near the Pebble Beach Golf Links. Other years there have been more Mercedes Gullwings

(continued)

In silver and crystal, the leading edge shows the automobile maker's nearly lost art (opposite), while enthusiasts carry on a tradition of tender care and expertise on their classics (below).

than were thought to exist, endless exhibits of Rolls Royces, "futuristic" displays of the few American dream cars to survive the 1950s and '60s, and the appearance of such rare automobiles as the Hispano-Suiza, the Delehaye and the Delage. Still, the Bugatti has been king at Pebble Beach, winning Best of Show seven times since 1950.

Always the connoisseur's choice, this world-class event reached a major new audience in 1990 when Ralph Lauren became the first household name to

(continued)

Classic car lovers swear that perfection is to be found in the details. Throughout the weekend of the Concours d'Elegance *there are details aplenty to savor front, back, and inside scores of unique vehicles.*

Awaiting their turn to be judged by the experts on the lawn between the Lodge and the Pacific, more modern models line up in a car buff's version of heaven's parking lot.

ever win at Pebble Beach. He did it with an immaculately restored Bugatti Type 57SC Atlantic that insiders said was worth more than $8 million. Of those who lingered long after the show was over, who will forget the day's final scene when Lauren returned to his cherished car, switched on the engine, patiently warmed it up and, as darkness fell, drove straight down the 18th fairway?

The next year Lauren did not enter a car, but he returned to Pebble Beach just to look. Dressed in his trademark faded jeans and jacket, he signed autographs from the balcony of his second-floor room overlooking the 18th green as an estimated 15,000 spectators roamed among the rows of classic cars below.

That's Pebble Beach.

At the climax of the Pebble Beach Concours d'Elegance, *winners with names like Rolls Royce and Pierce Arrow take their places, and those who have dressed in the manner of a more gracious era take theirs* (opposite).

"A garden for generations to enjoy."
— S.F.B. MORSE

A Bounty of Elegance
On a Rough-hewn Shore

Rich in style and tradition, Pebble Beach is an entity set apart from the everyday world. It is exclusive and yet accessible. Pebble Beach resorts, private residences, golf courses and the incomparable beauty of the land give a feeling of timelessness, a retreat from the outside. Its lifestyle, with its self-indulging amenities, is unlike any resort in the world: a tradition in elegance.

From the earliest planning Pebble Beach was destined to be a golf resort. The challenge was in giving protection to an environment that had evolved over millions of years through a passage of time that has never been fully explored or understood. The gradual placement of golf courses, resorts and homes has been in response to what nature had already provided. By example, Pebble Beach Golf Links is a reverent comment to the landscape, and the Links at Spanish Bay, with its restoration of dunes and native plants, is testimony to the shoreline's natural past.

Under other, less-concerned stewardship the natural beauty of Pebble Beach could have been forever lost. But instead the rugged coastline with the Lone Cypress standing as sentinel, the Del Monte Forest and its rare plant and animal life, 17-Mile Drive, the golf courses, resorts and private homes are symbols of a legacy to be carried forward into the future.

Pebble Beach tradition, however, is not captured in a time capsule and buried under a cornerstone. The roots of this tradition extend well back to an earlier period when the highest of standards were first set, and those

The casual lifestyle at Pebble Beach is a treasure which is shared by both residents and visitors.

One of the most elegant features of The Lodge at Pebble Beach is the Library Card Room, a private dining area on the main floor.

principles remain constant to this day, the Pebble Beach experience changes to meet the demands of the visitor, adjusting from generation to generation.

The Inn at Spanish Bay, which opened in the fall of 1987, especially reflects this philosophy. In contrast to the venerable Lodge at Pebble Beach and its link to the past, the Inn speaks to the present.

Flanked by groves of tall Monterey pines and facing Spanish Bay and the Pacific, the Inn is an architectural blending of Spanish and Old Monterey styles. The lobby, with its overscale sofas, black leather chairs, touches of wrought iron, flower arrangements and a huge granite fireplace, is earthy yet casually classic in its California style. The lobby punctuates the welcoming statement for the entire Inn.

The theme is carried from the public areas into the guest rooms, which are also furnished with oversized sofas and chairs, fireplaces and framed artwork. All rooms have fireplaces, most have balconies and the fourth-floor "dormer" rooms have architectural designs that create an unusual and cozy atmosphere. In all, there are 270 rooms, including mini-suites with sitting rooms and three luxury suites—Hospitality, Governor's and Presidential.

But the public areas—the restaurants, lounges and retail shops—are the travelers' crossroads. There is nightly entertainment in the Lobby Lounge, where refreshments and cocktails are served either outdoors or inside by the giant fireplace. Traps is a warm, friendly cocktail lounge with complimentary hors d'oeuvres and televised sports. The Dunes, the Inn's main dining room, features spectacular views of the golf course and Spanish Bay and superb selections of California cuisine. The Bay Club, an elegantly-appointed dinner restaurant, offers excellent Northern Italian cuisine.

The retail shops range from Breezes, carrying sundries, resort wear and gift selections, to Elan, an upscale women's boutique, to the tennis and golf pro shops. Health and fitness facilities, including outdoor swimming pool, instructors, weight room, aerobics classes and sauna are at the Spanish Bay Club, which also has a cocktail lounge and dining room for casual breakfast and lunch.

The Tennis Pavilion has eight outdoor courts, including a stadium court for tournament play and two lighted courts, a pro shop, lockers and professional instruction.

The Inn at Spanish Bay and the Links at Spanish Bay may be the "new traditionalists" of the Pebble Beach resort family, but by following example they radiate a feeling of entrenchment, of being in place. In emulation, what more perfect example could there be than The Lodge at Pebble Beach?

Stately in grandeur, resplendent in setting, The Lodge is the benevolent seignior of its vast estate. Its architecture contains Spanish and Italian influence, embraced by stone, tiles, marbles and mosaics and framed by French windows and doors and a "promenade de luxe" balcony terrace. The main structure, with just 11 guest rooms on the upper floor, is the ceremonial keeper of the grounds, giving no hint at its entrance of the superb vista awaiting the viewer.

To walk through the outer lobby, down the steps and into the Terrace Lounge is to transcend from one world into another. Only after following this short, carpeted path, does the spectacular view unfold. There, through the tall French-pane windows and in glorious panorama, is the green of Pebble Beach's 18th fairway, the blue expanse of Carmel Bay, the dark-green skyline silhouette of Point Lobos, and beyond, the northernmost coastal ridges of the Santa Lucia Range.

Old-world elegance is seen in each of The Lodge's 161 guest rooms. The rooms, almost all with wood-burning fireplaces, are spacious and designed to satisfy personal comfort. There are muted shell tones in California style, but with a European flair, and the furnishings would fit easily into any home.

Despite its natural setting and stately ambience, The Lodge is, first and foremost, a busy hotel. Taking a glance at some of the Lodge's "vital statistics" gives some idea of why it competes in complexity and size with any urban hostelry:

• The Lodge at Pebble Beach wine cellar houses over 11,000 bottles of domestic and imported wines; The Inn at Spanish Bay wine cellar holds 8,000 bottles. The combined consumption of wine by guests at The Lodge and The Inn is between 10,000 and 12,000 bottles a year.

• The Pebble Beach Company recycles 4,000 pounds of glass and cardboard each week.

• The Lodge serves 155,125 individual dessert and breakfast pastries yearly. Chefs annually use 4,380 gallons of whipping cream.

• A total of 31,200 pounds of meat and fowl and 18,250 pounds of fish are

The Lodge, the quintessential symbol of quality, has been welcoming discerning guests from the world over since 1919.

A stylish circular driveway provides the entrance to the Inn at Spanish Bay (above). Swimmers have a choice of the outdoor pool or the Pacific Ocean at the Beach and Tennis Club (right). The home of boats (below) is owned by the Robert Louis Stevenson School.

cooked each year in The Lodge kitchen.

• There are 1,206 full-time, 49 part-time, 25 full-time temporaries and 65 "on call" employees in the Pebble Beach Company. There are more than 500 different job assignments. Here are a few:

On the front line with guests are: doormen, bell captain, valets, concierge, golf shop assistants, tennis hostesses, desk clerks, bartenders, servers, waiters and waitresses.

That's just the surface. Other jobs include: honor bar and turndown attendants, security, housekeepers, housemen, buspersons, bakers, hotel engineers, lead cooks, bakers, *sous* chefs, butchers, shuttledrivers, lobby attendants and fitness instructors.

That's typical of a hotel. More unusual jobs include: tree climber, florist, sign painter, potwasher, pasta maker, griddle cook, saucier, office clerk, silver steward, seamstress, marble technician, and of course golf professionals, such as golf cart mechanic, duneskeeper, road crewmen, electrician, divot topdresser and greenskeepers.

• During a typical AT&T Pebble Beach National Pro-Am week, 40,000 pounds of ice are used in addition to what the in-house ice machines churn out. To keep the ice and other ingredients flowing, an extra 30 bartenders, 30 waitresses, 20 bussers, 10 "bar backs" and 11 cashiers are hired.

• About 125,000 plastic cups are used at the AT&T. Guests consume 5,000 pounds of beef, 6,000 pounds of seafood, 8,000 hamburger buns, 12,000 soft drinks, 18,000 cans of beer, 9,000 pounds of various groceries and 2,000 pounds of coffee.

• The Pebble Beach *Concours d'Elegance*, held in August, beats the Pro-Am in ice used by 10,000 pounds.

• Between 150 and 200 ice carvings are made each year at each hotel.

• The main switchboard at The Lodge at Pebble Beach receives 545,000 incoming calls a year.

• In addition to delivering a daily newspaper to each occupied room at The Lodge every weekday, 10 copies of six different daily newspapers are delivered to The Lodge concierge desk each day, as are 30 copies of The Sunday New York Times. The Inn at Spanish Bay orders a daily newspaper for each occupied room, plus 20 copies of five different dailies for its concierge desk.

• Pebble Beach Golf Links is fed 45 tons of fertilizer a year and 18 tons of lawn seed.

• Sod for Pebble Beach Golf Links is grown on a three-quarter-acre plot which is turned over twice, equaling 65,000 square feet of sod a year.

• It takes 51,840 man hours a year to maintain Pebble Beach Golf Course. This includes a mechanic, superintendent, assistant superintendent, field foreman, field superintendent and irrigation technician.

• More than 250,000 trees and shrubs are grown on-site each year for landscaping the resorts, golf courses and Del Monte Forest land owned by

Pebble Beach Company. There are 12 endangered plant species, including the Menzies wallflower, Beach Layia and Tidestrom's Lupine.

The Lodge is a refuge, a retreat for travelers but it is also a stage for social gatherings, creating a form of theater and a sense of drama. The Terrace Lounge by day is a loge seat for one of the best shows nature provides: the Monterey Peninsula. After dark, with lights accenting the pines off the 18th green, the Terrace Lounge becomes an intimate cocktail setting where guests meet to visit and listen to live and light jazz before dining in the adjacent Cypress Room or downstairs in Club XIX.

The Cypress Room provides the same view as the Terrace Lounge, giving it the distinction of being an attractive choice for breakfast, lunch or dinner.

But the Lodge's main dining room does not rest on the quality of its view; the fresh seafood dishes are superb and fortunate is the guest who dines on a day when lobster strudel is a specialty.

Club XIX, downstairs and also looking out across the lawn to the 18th green, is a first class lunch and dinner restaurant that has not forgotten its heritage of fine French sauces. The tiny but elegant bar has long been considered one of the best 19th holes in golf.

The Tap Room, on the main floor, is the informal clubhouse to the Pebble Beach Golf Links, rich in golf history and conviviality. Throughout the years golfers of great stature and great enthusiasm have stopped at the Tap Room to relax and recount their latest round. The colorful golfing history of Pebble

The Inn at Spanish Bay opened in 1987 with 270 rooms. It has a Spanish-style architecture with a touch of Old Monterey, personified by the luxurious lobby (above). At dusk, a bagpiper plays across the links (left).

Seafood comes in all types and flavors along Fisherman's Wharf.

Beach Golf Links has been preserved in the vintage photos of prominent players set against a background of dark-green felt walls and wood paneling. This is Pebble Beach's relaxed and comfortable pub.

Opposite the entrance to the Lodge are the shopping arcade, the Gallery restaurant and bar and the Pebble Beach golf shop. The breezeway contains more than 15 retail shops carrying selections in the finest fashionwear, sportswear, accessories, specialty items and gifts.

A short walk or drive along the golf course, through the passage between the fourth tee on the left and the 17th tee on the right, is the Beach & Tennis Club. Perched on the cliffs above Stillwater Cove, it is completely surrounded by the golf links. This private club, with 14 tennis courts and pro shop, heated outdoor pool, fitness facilities and dining room overlooking the 17th hole, is available to guests of the Lodge.

What makes great resorts like the Lodge at Pebble Beach and the Inn at Spanish Bay are the people. Travelers from everywhere have ventured to Pebble Beach. The attraction, of course, is the incomparable beauty and the challenge of championship courses but Pebble Beach is more than a golf

outing in an unmatched setting. It harbors those seeking anonymity, offering privacy to both the famous and the reclusive, respectful of the personal desires of all guests but also providing sociability if preferred.

Surprisingly, not everyone comes to Pebble Beach to play golf. Recreation and exercise at Pebble Beach also take the form of horseback riding, swimming and other kinds of exercise such as tennis, walking, jogging and bicycling along 17-Mile Drive.

A private toll road within Del Monte Forest which curves around the most scenic shoreline of the Monterey Peninsula, 17-Mile Drive was first used by horse and buggy drivers and was opened to automobiles in the early 1900s. It was an instant and lasting success, ideal for sunset-watching, with picnic areas, secluded beaches and open vistas of the Pacific Ocean.

For the more active, bicycles may be rented at the concierge desks. The most popular cycling—and combined sightseeing—is on the level sections of 17-Mile Drive, along the coast. Typical rides are about seven miles and resort guests can arrange for a shuttle to return them to their hotel.

The Pebble Beach Equestrian Center is about a half-mile from the Lodge.

Pedestrians and bicyle riders share the path along the old railroad tracks.

Victorian houses built in the late 1880s add a touch of nostalgia to Pacific Grove. Beacon House (far left) and Green Gables (at left) are among the best known. Green Gables is now a bed and breakfast establishment. Above: a durable old gingerbread house with a multi-colored roof that has withstood the passage of time.

Never mind the sign, the fish are biting on the Wharf (above), while the exterior of an early cannery (right) still survives on historic Cannery Row.

Private lessons are available by appointment and escorted trail rides are offered twice daily. There are over 34 miles of trails within Del Monte Forest.

The roads of Del Monte Forest, particularly 17-Mile Drive, are among the most scenic anywhere. Walkers create their own routes by following maps obtained at the concierge desks or signs along the roads.

Activities and sightseeing within Del Monte Forest are just part of the adventure. In addition to Pebble Beach, the Monterey Peninsula is a composite of seven cities with household names such as Carmel and Monterey. Vast unincorporated areas nearby are equally famous: Big Sur and Carmel Valley.

MONTEREY

Monterey is the acknowledged birthplace of the Monterey Peninsula and has retained much of the flavor of its Spanish forefathers. It was here that Father Junipero Serra in 1770 established the second of 21 Catholic missions. It was here in 1846 that the United States flag was raised over the Custom House and it was also here that the California State Constitution was drafted in 1849.

In 1879 a chapter in a compelling love story was played out when 29-

Peninsula fishermen maintain the old tradition of mending their nets near the Wharf at Custom House Plaza.

year-old Robert Louis Stevenson came to Monterey in pursuit of Fanny Osbourne, 10 years his senior and mother of three children. The Stevenson House, where the author of *Treasure Island* stayed during a portion of his courtship, is one of the many romantic and historic abodes open to public tour. Stevenson and Fanny finally married, but not until she had led him on a trip that took them from Monterey through the Napa Valley and onto the South Pacific.

Monterey was also a thriving seaport, first as a port of call for whaling ships and commercial vessels in the 1840s and a century later as the sardine industry capital of California. Nobel Prize-winning author John Steinbeck set Monterey's Cannery Row as the backdrop for his famous novel by the same name. Steinbeck also used it as the setting for *Sweet Thursday* and *Tortilla Flat*.

The city's favorite attractions are Fisherman's Wharf, Cannery Row and Monterey Bay Aquarium. New to the wharf are the Stanton History Center and Allen Knight Maritime Museum, which are scheduled to open in the fall of 1992.

Monterey's historic tie to the sea is best seen at Fisherman's Wharf and the adjacent Custom House. Fisherman's Wharf has changed little over the years. Although the fishermen rarely mend their nets there, preferring the more expansive nearby plaza, a visitor can still find the flavor of the old days. Fish markets cater to the local residents, fine seafood restaurants offer quality fare and charter boats provide a chance to catch a salmon in season or spy a gray whale migrating to Baja California.

Pacific Grove also claims the Monterey Bay Aquarium although it was built on the site of a former sardine cannery that straddled the Monterey-Pacific Grove city limit. For many, the Aquarium is a destination in itself, home to virtually every known species of sea life found in Monterey Bay. As the canyon in the bay continues to be explored, the Aquarium keeps track of

those species that require the darkness and water pressure of the depths, even though they cannot be displayed. Special exhibits have included whales, sharks and jellyfish. There are hands-on exhibits, a kelp tank with schools of fish, live "feedings," videos of the canning days and sea otters at play in a special display tank. There is also a trout stream and a manmade tide pool that can't be distinguished from the real thing. Drawing nearly two million visitors a year, it is popular with both children and adults.

Between Fisherman's Wharf and the Monterey Bay Aquarium is Cannery Row. This is the old sardine cannery district popularized by Steinbeck. Today it's a revitalized shopping and restaurant strip that's fun for everyone.

There is plenty of romantic history on Cannery Row—both in real form

Two Monterey landmarks: the Carmel Mission (left), second oldest in California, founded in 1770 by Father Junipero Serra, whose body lies there, and the Bird Rock telescopes (above) on 17-Mile Drive.

*Visitors find diverse shops at the Pebble Beach
Arcade* (left) *and in a Carmel alleyway*
(above), *and members find good food in the
Cypress Point Club dining room* (below).

and in the aura of Steinbeck's stories. One place to start is Ed Ricketts' lab. A marine biologist, Ricketts was "Doc" in *Cannery Row*. His lab still stands at 800 Cannery Row. It's a private club now, but it looks just as it did when Steinbeck and Ricketts gave parties there—both real and fictitious.

PACIFIC GROVE

Known by its residents as "The Last Hometown," Pacific Grove started as a Methodist retreat in 1875. That influence has remained in this town of Victorian homes. It wasn't until 1969, for example, that its blue laws were discarded and over-the-counter liquor went on sale. There are no bars in Pacific Grove, unless they are accompanied by a restaurant.

As its nickname implies, Pacific Grove is a family town. Its activities, such as Good Old Days, the Butterfly Parade, California High School Band Competition, Annual Wildflower Show at the Pacific Grove Museum and Feast of Lanterns are generally planned for residents and kids. The museum was originally built by Pacific Improvement Co., predecessor of S.F.B. Morse's Del Monte Properties, and is considered one of the finest municipally-owned museums in the country.

Pacific Grove has a city-owned waterfront and marine reserve that stretch for more than five miles. It's a popular bicycle and jogging path, a place to view the monarch butterflies and the municipal golf course with ocean views.

The bicycle and jogging path is also used by couples out for a walk, families with a stroller and individuals watching the waves. It begins by the Pacific, passes Lover's Point, a small promontory with a sweeping view of the bay (and where one can occasionally see young surfers taking advantage of the waves that curve around the point) and heads for the Monterey Bay Aquarium. The path, which follows a former Southern Pacific right-of-way, continues through Cannery Row and Monterey, passing by the Old Hotel Del Monte on its way to Marina, just northeast of the Peninsula.

The bright orange and black monarch butterflies migrate to Pacific Grove seasonally, resting in various eucalyptus groves. The butterfly is protected; there are signs warning of penalties for harming them.

CARMEL

Carmel has for years been a favorite of vacationers who like courtyard shopping, walks on the beach and dinner for two.

The village's full name is Carmel-by-the-Sea, and it has good reason to brag about the hyphenations. Its main street, Ocean Ave., ends at one of the world's most scenic white beaches. There are no fast-food concessions or roller coasters here. This beach is as pristine as it was when discovered in 1602 and the day the city was incorporated in 1916. The mile-long stretch of fine grain sand is perfect for beachcombing, tide pooling below the ninth and 10th fairways of the Pebble Beach Golf Links, playing volleyball, beginning and intermediate surfing or just sunning and watching people go by.

Carmel has been home to the famous since its origin. Robinson Jeffers discovered the beauty of the area in the early 1900s and wrote much of his poetry at Tor House, the home he built near Carmel Point. Others to follow included Sinclair Lewis, Mary Austin, George Sterling, Jean Arthur and, more than 25 years ago, Clint Eastwood.

With 65 art galleries all within easy walking distance, Carmel is the art center of California's central coast. Artists first came to Carmel in 1903, responding to advertisements sent to the "School Teachers of California and other Brain Workers." As an incentive to living and working in Carmel the artists were offered building lots for $100 or less.

Artists continued to come to Carmel after the San Francisco earthquake and fire of 1906, seeking refuge and studios. Since those early years artists of all mediums have made Carmel their home.

Protector of its early image as an artist's retreat, Carmel has what city dwellers would call odd laws and policies. Neon signs are forbidden. So are sidewalks, except in the main shopping section downtown. There is no house-to-house mail delivery. Homes have names instead of street numbers.

Carmel Mission, where Pope John Paul II came to pray, is an excellent example of California's restored missions.

Carmel Valley

Carmel Valley is the rural arm of the Monterey Peninsula, but its bucolic charm threatens now to change its rural character. That's the paradox of this beautiful, narrow valley that runs inland from Carmel Bay.

Once a regional farming district and home to those who had the time and money to live away from the core of the Peninsula, it has gradually become suburbia to upper-income professionals while keeping its rural appearance. Its main attraction is sun.

During the summer months Carmel Valley is usually 15 degrees or more warmer than the other cities on the Monterey Peninsula. The reason is the fog that settles along the coast. The fog keeps towns like Pacific Grove cool, but rarely stretches far enough—or long enough—inland to dampen the spirits in Carmel Valley.

Big Sur Highway

This is America's Amalfi. Built by prison labor, the narrow two-lane road opened in 1937 and has been desperately clinging to the steep sides of the Santa Lucia range ever since.

Driving south, the passenger feels virtually suspended in midair on the tight curves. Over 400 feet below, the Pacific crashes against the jagged

Fishing boats set out for their daily catch in the waters of Monterey Bay on the northern end of the Peninsula.

rocks of the cliffs. The whole scene can be unnerving but not enough to prevent the road from becoming one of the most popular drives in the U.S. In the mid-1960s, Big Sur Highway was named the first scenic highway in the country.

The rewards for driving this stretch of Highway 1 from Carmel to San Simeon are as immense as the mountains and ocean it threads. The rugged coastline is awesome in its dive to the ocean surface, and the redwood groves hidden in tight, fern-carpeted canyons are majestic.

About 30 miles south of Carmel the highway curves slightly inland, away from the ocean. Here among the redwoods is the village called Big Sur. Camping and hiking are available for lovers of the outdoors, and for the lovers of views there are Ventana and Nepenthe, two patio dining spots high above the Pacific.

Because of the Monterey Peninsula's mild climate, nothing is out of season. Recreational sports are played year round. The more passive activities of walking, hiking, biking, beachcombing, sightseeing, shopping and

just appreciating the magnificent scenery are always present. But the Monterey Peninsula is known as a vacation destination, and for a vast number of visitors to the area, that can only mean one thing: a chance to play some of the world's best golf.

Visitors come to the Monterey Peninsula and the surrounding area 365 days a year to enjoy the pleasures described above and more. There is a sense of serenity among the cypress groves and on the coastline that can't be found at more urbanized, "developed," manmade resort areas. That may be the greatest attraction of the place for both visitors and residents. The experience of Monterey is casual, close to nature, relaxed and active.

There are 18 golf courses on the Peninsula, six private, nine open to the public and three military. Their degree of difficulty ranges from the relatively hospitable Old Del Monte Golf Course to the ever-difficult Spyglass Hill Golf Course, always one of the toughest challenges on the PGA tour, to the incredible Pebble Beach Golf Links. Every golfer's dream is to play a paradise called Pebble Beach.

The Californian (left and above) *is California's official ambassador tall ship. The gaff-rigged topsail schooner travels the coast to educate and entertain adults and children.*

THE GOLF COURSES

What is there about the Monterey Peninsula that produces such an abundance of quality golf courses? Cypress Point is No. 3, Pebble Beach No. 5 in GOLF DIGEST's ranking of America's 100 Greatest Courses. Spyglass Hill and The Links at Spanish Bay are also in the top 100. Those four are included among the top 15 in California—Cypress Point in first place and Pebble Beach in second. The other Peninsula courses are also excellent and, like the Big Four, the fortuitous results of a mixture of the natural beauty of the land, favorable weather and great architects.

*The Masterpiece that Sprung
From the Will of Samuel
Morse and the Drawing
Board of Jack Neville.*

PEBBLE BEACH
GOLF LINKS

The rugged and scenic landscape comprising Pebble Beach today was, for a very long time, a golf course waiting to be built. Samuel Morse knew that, and Pebble Beach was something special from the moment it opened in 1919, designed by Jack Neville with bunkering assistance from Douglas Grant. Its total cost was $75,000, one of the great golf bargains of all time.

Neville's primary task was to get in as many holes along the water as possible. He wound up with eight, sited principally along the craggy headlands overlooking Stillwater Cove and Carmel Bay, and the Pacific shoreline, where he routed the two dramatic finishing holes.

Pebble Beach has been hosting important tournaments since 1929, but mostly it's known simply as a great place to play golf.

1

Par 4

373 Yards

It has been called the ideal opening hole. The first hole doglegs gently to the right at about the tee-shot landing area, flanked by Lodge rooms on the right and luxurious estates on the left. Because of the fairway bunker on the left just ahead of where the hole swings right, most players are wary of using a driver off the tee, going with either a 3-wood or long iron. A medium iron will put you on a green where one first experiences that, at Pebble Beach, most putts break toward the ocean.

2

Par 5

502 Yards

From the back tee, the second provides the best birdie opportunity on the course, although when a birdie becomes almost a necessity to stay with the field sudden thorns seem to emerge. The hole contains six fairway bunkers, with a wide barranca bisecting the fairway about 75 yards short of the green. In sudden death at the 1977 PGA Championship, Lanny Wadkins' 2nd shot got a fortunate bounce off the green bank allowing him to birdie this hole and stay tied with his opponent, Gene Littler.

3

Par 4

388 Yards

The third wraps around a wooded barranca on the left, and heads downhill toward the ocean. A slight hook on a long drive will leave a short iron to the green. Jack Nicklaus hit a sand wedge 15 feet from the pin to birdie this hole in the final round of the 1982 U.S. Open. But don't let the green fool you. While it appears to slope away from the ocean, because of the downhill layout, the break is actually toward the ocean. It was here in the 1977 PGA Championship that Lanny Wadkins won in sudden death when Gene Littler bogied.

4

Par 4

327 Yards

On the scorecard the fourth, 327 yards from the tips and barely 300 from the regular tees, has all the credentials of a birdie hole. And you do see a number of birdies here, in the AT&T Pebble Beach National Pro-Am and in the U.S. Open. The problems, however, are a predatory extension of a huge fairway trap, partially obscured by trees, on the left and a fairway that slopes toward the shoreline on the far right. The green has been rebuilt, expanded considerably from the previous bowl shape that had grown from decades of shots out of the surrounding greenside bunkers.

5

Par 3

166 Yards

They once called the 166-yard fifth the only dogleg par 3 in the world. Trimming some of the huge and protruding trees on the right and left effectively straightened the hole, which runs uphill through a narrow chute between the trees with a large, menacing bunker directly in front of the green. The green has been completely rebuilt and a complex heating system, which warms the soil through underground tubes, was installed to facilitate the growing of grass. Along with all the other trouble, there is out-of-bounds on both the left and right.

6

Par 5

516 Yards

Here is where the course launches a five-hole odyssey along the cliff-tops, with water coming into play for the first time. It's a dramatic par 5, dropping down off the tee and then sweeping uphill to an exposed green overlooking Stillwater Cove far below. The pros feel they should reach the green in two, but the second is often a blind shot and the green is well protected by three bunkers, two on the right side to catch a faded second shot. Most Pebble Beach aficionados claim this is where the course really begins.

7

Par 3

107 Yards

Along with the 16th at Cypress Point and the 12th at Augusta National, the seventh at Pebble Beach ranks among the three most notable par-3 holes in golf. It measures just over 100 yards and tumbles downhill from the elevated tee to the rebuilt green jutting out into the corner of Carmel Bay. The key element here is the wind. It gusts and swirls to the point where the tee shot can vary from a half wedge to a full 5-iron. Occasionally it reaches the point where you need a 3-iron to hit the green, as Ken Venturi did when he won the Crosby in 1960.

8

Par 4

431 Yards

Jack Neville's mouth must have watered when he first saw the landscape that would become the eighth hole at Pebble Beach. A blind tee shot that carries to the edge of a cliff sets up a spectacular approach of some 190 yards over a yawning chasm to a tiny green 100 feet below, protected by traps on three sides. The rough around the green is heavy, as Jack Nicklaus discovered in the final round of the 1982 U.S. Open when his string of five straight birdies was ended by a bogey on eight. You can bail out on the second shot by sweeping around to the left, playing for a five to avoid a six.

9

Par 4

464 Yards

Despite the menacing features of the eighth hole, there are those who claim the ninth is the toughest on the course. It's easy to understand why. The ninth is 464 yards of a sliver-like fairway extending along the Carmel Bay shoreline. A fairway bunker on the left discourages any tee shots from taking the high road through the rough.

10

Par 4

426 Yards

Just when you've survived the rigors of the ninth hole, Pebble Beach makes you do it all over again on 10. It's not quite as long as nine, but it has the same basic characteristics, sweeping majestically along the headland and culminating in another small green tucked away in the remote southeast corner of the course. Tom Watson made a miracle par here in the final round of the 1982 Open. He hit his second shot over the cliff to a shelf below the green, pitched up out of the rough and holed a 25-foot putt.

11

Par 4

384 Yards

With the water holes out of the way for the next hour and a half, Pebble Beach turns inland at the 11th tee and starts the long trek back to the Lodge. The hole slides slightly to the right, leading to a green that is oddly shaped at a 45-degree angle. What makes the 11th a tough hole is that it plays uphill and therefore considerably longer than its 384 yards, and has out-of-bounds on the right. In tournament play you seldom see much of a gallery on this hole, because nobody wants to walk that far. It's easier to slip on over from the 10th tee to the 13th tee.

12

Par 3

202 Yards

From the tee, particularly to the amateur golfer, the 12th has a ferocious appearance. As par 3s go it's no monster, 184 yards from the regular tees and 202 from the tips, but the greenside bunkering conveys the distinct impression that only a perfect tee shot will reach and hold on the green. This, of course, is only a delusion but it is in the golfer's mind nevertheless. There are problems, in addition to the bunkers. Balls kicking left off the green wind up in thick rough. Sometimes you have to look hard for them. Balls too far on the right are out-of-bounds.

13

Par 4

392 Yards

Here is the breather we've waited for since the first hole. It's relatively flat, just 392 yards from the back tees, with no bunkering either in front or to the left of the green. A middle handicapper can reasonably expect to have a go at a par. However, there is a massive bunker running parallel to the rising fairway on the left; there are three bunkers to the right of the green, all in perfect position to catch a faded second and the slick green suggests you keep the ball below the hole.

14

Par 5

565 Yards

Unless they have a typhoon tailwind even the longest of the pros consider this a legitimate three-shot hole. It's a great par 5 with lovely gardens all along the right side that are, of course, out-of-bounds. It's easy to ricochet a tee shot off the trees into those gardens. Two substantial traps protect a two-level green that produces large numbers of three-putts.

15

Par 4

397 Yards

A succesful tee shot here is played right to left through the window over an ominous barranca. Golfers hitting that shot are rewarded by a wide, hazard-free fairway. The second area of trouble is around the green, guarded diligently by four bunkers, the first on the right about 40 yards short. Smart golf: leave yourself an uphill putt. A down-hiller may roll right off the green.

16

Par 4

402 Yards

Although the hole looks open and inviting from the tee, trees are the peril on 16. The trees that may have escaped your gaze initially are located in clusters, to the right of the tee-shot landing area, partly concealing a deadly barranca, and, most importantly, on both sides of the green. The greenside groves are so thick that they affect an approach shot that is just off line, particularly from the left side of the fairway. Hale Irwin made a stunning birdie from the center fairway bunker to win the playoff in the 1984 Crosby.

17

Par 3

209 Yards

Is there another hole anywhere that can claim two historical shots that occurred on the 71st hole of the U.S. Open, resulting in a victory for each of the perpetrators? Nicklaus hit his famous 1-iron that wound up almost leaning on the flag in 1972 and Watson lobbed in a perilous pitch from deep rough in 1982. Dramatic stuff, but the fact is that 17 is a gnawingly difficult par 3, 209 yards into the prevailing ocean wind, with a two-tiered hourglass green linked by a humpback. Beyond the green: sand, rocks and the world's largest water hazard.

18

Par 5

548 Yards

The only way to fully appreciate the 18th at Pebble Beach is to play it. The view from the tee is awesome: rugged shoreline hugging the fairway all along the left side, rocks forming a buffer between the grass and the namesake beach; homes on the right side with out-of-bounds stakes in their front yards; and trees partially blocking the entrance from the right to a green flanked on three sides by bunkers.

SPYGLASS HILL GOLF COURSE

This long, demanding course, designed by Robert Trent Jones and opened in 1966, can be unforgiving. One of three courses in play for the AT&T Pebble Beach National Pro-Am, it almost always produces the highest scoring average of the tournament. The first five holes wind through sand dunes and offer magnificent ocean views. The next 13 are cut through pine forests. The large, undulating greens are protected by ponds on three par 5s. The names given to each of the holes were derived from Robert Louis Stevenson's classic, *Treasure Island,* including such beauties as the first hole, called "Treasure Island" because the green is actually an island in the sand, the 14th called "Long John Silver" because it's a double-dogleg par 5, and the infamous par-4 16th, known as "Black Dog."

Ask any pro or amateur who has played this course and he will warn you: always to treat it with the respect it deserves.

Part Pine Valley and part Pebble Beach, Spyglass Hill exudes a split personality. Robert Trent Jones, who still considers it one of his authentic masterpieces, routed the first five holes through the rolling oceanside dunesland and the last 13 through the towering pine forests. "It's two shots tougher than Pebble," said Bing Crosby when it opened in 1966. You get a quick first impression of Spyglass, which starts with a 600-yard hole to an island green in a sea of sand.

The par-3 fifth at Spyglass Hill gives great advantage to the player who knows its dangers. Miss the green and you're in wasteland; on the green a valley channels shots front and center.

Among the challenges at the second hole (above) are a fairway wasteland and a climb from the first green to the elevated tee.

The 12th is a classic Peninsula par 3, 180 yards from the back tees with a pond on the left and a hazard on the right.

Spyglass turns inland with the sixth hole, an uphill dogleg right into the woods that seems to play longer than 415 yards.

Water comes into play left of the green on the 515-yard seventh (**right**), which also has a couple of busy fairway bunkers.

Black-tailed deer are a protected species at Spyglass, often emerging from their homes in the woods to cross fairways.

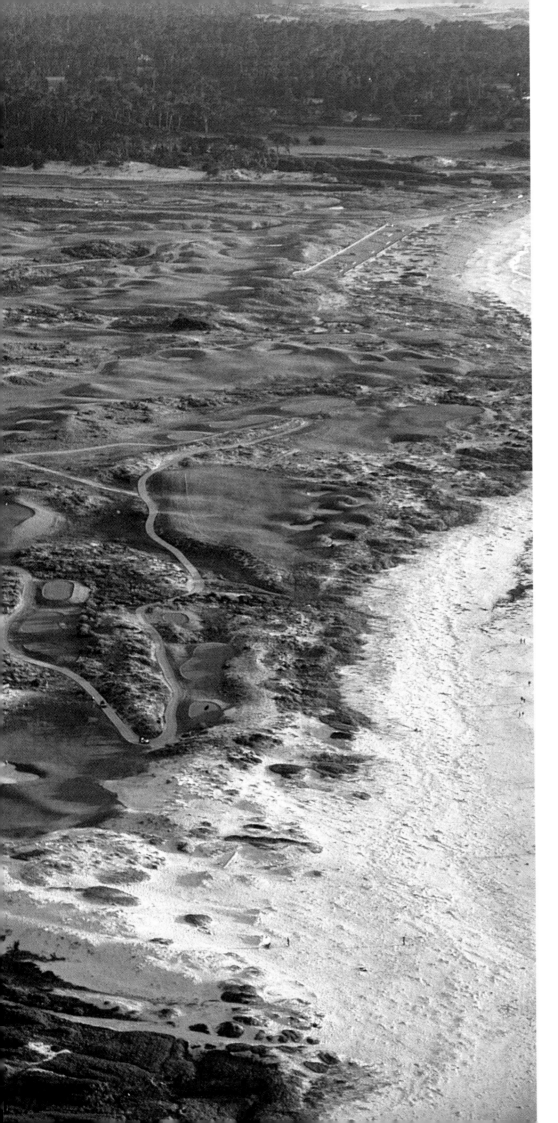

A $6 Million Touch of Scotland Complete with Sand Dunes, Mossy Hummocks and Fescue Grass.

THE LINKS AT SPANISH BAY

Robert Trent Jones Jr., Tom Watson and Frank (Sandy) Tatum combined talents and insights to design The Links at Spanish Bay, which opened in 1987. Fast-rolling and tailored in the true Scottish fashion, it has fescue grass fairways and greens, pot bunkers and mounds. Unlike traditional U.S. layouts the links requires run-up shots. Considering that all but four holes are near the ocean this tactic is especially advantageous when the wind kicks up, which it often does.

Most of the holes are bordered by sand and by natural vegetation indigenous to the region, making accuracy a must. Large expanses of sand dunes up to 24 feet in height and covered with native grasses and plants characterize the course. The back nine is particularly enjoyable. It features a par-4 12th, a short par-3 13th giving a spectacular view corridor to the ocean and a difficult par-4 17th.

Dunes, pot bunkers and a clear view of the Pacific Ocean comprise the ideal tone-setter for the 500-yard first hole (left) of The Links at Spanish Bay.

Patterned after the Road Hole at St. Andrews with three fairway bunkers, the 459-yard fifth (right) is the most difficult test on the front nine.

The par-4 third at Spanish Bay (left) is called "Pitch and Run" and that's how the wise golfer should play his approach shot on this dogleg-left hole.

The rugged natural beauty of Spanish Bay is symbolized by the par-4 sixth (top left) which has 10 bunkers, the par-4 ninth (middle left) with out-of-bounds on the right, and the par-3 16th (left) near the ocean.

The long and narrow par-5 18th (above) requires a third shot hit over a salty marsh to the green.

Woods, Wildlife and Water Give the New Kid on the Tour the Natural Look of its Neighbors.

POPPY HILLS GOLF COURSE

The creation of Robert Trent Jones Jr., Poppy Hills opened in 1986 under the ownership of the Northern California Golf Association. It is a long and tight course with lots of trees, water and sand. Many of the greens are flanked by chipping areas, which give the player the option to chip or putt. On most holes, the option also exists to either play it safe or go for broke, especially on the par-5 ninth and 18th holes. Poppy Hills joined Pebble Beach Golf Links and Spyglass Hill Golf Course in 1991 as a rotation course for the annual AT&T Pebble Beach National Pro-Am.

Framed by ancient stands of Monterey Pines, the par-3 17th at Poppy Hills (below) offers an inviting target from the white tees.

The late-afternoon views at Poppy Hills are memorable, highlighted by a dramatic sunset over the Pacific (right) and the lengthening shadows on the wooded 500-yard 18th (below).

There are Those Who Believe
Cypress Point to be the Most
Beautiful Course in the World.

CYPRESS POINT CLUB

This spectacular course is the best-known Western work of the Scottish architect Alister Mackenzie, who designed it in 1928. With sand and sea seemingly on all sides, Mackenzie made the most of its natural resources. The greens are fast and undulating.

High winds make the finishing holes the toughest on this course.

The famous par-3 16th hole requires a 200-yard carry over an ocean gorge. This is the hole tour pro "Porky" Oliver once took 16 strokes to finish but it's also been aced six times.

A bird's-eye view is the best way to savor the majesty of Cypress Point and portions of Pebble Beach (below). The sixth at Cypress (right) weaves a 518-yard ribbon through the forests.

You can risk cutting the drive over the dogleg on the 363-yard eighth at Cypress Point (top), but the landing area is small and the dunes lie in wait to devour the failed shot.

The 13th is the truest links-style hole at Cypress, (above) with no trees and a 180-yard carry over the dunes off the tee. You're also playing straight into the prevailing wind.

One of Cypress Point's hidden gems is the short 15th (left), overshadowed by its neighbor the 16th, but a spectacular hole with the tee shot carrying over a yawning chasm.

Accuracy is the key on the 18th (below), requiring shots through and over the cypress trees. Downwind from the white tees (329 yards) the game's longest drivers can reach the green.

There are few more magnificent holes, or views, in golf than the 16th, 231 yards from the back tees over an inlet of the Pacific to a green guarded by ice plant.

The Peninsula's Senior Citizen was Created Long Before the Birth of Pebble Beach.

OLD DEL MONTE GOLF COURSE

Designed by Charles Maud, Old Del Monte is the oldest golf course west of the Mississippi. It was built in 1897 and was the first course in the world to have green fairways throughout the year. An inland course, Old Del Monte offers a meandering, hilly layout with lots of trees. It was the original host of the California State Amateur back in 1912 and contintues to host flights of this Championship each year.

Open to the public and operated by the Pebble Beach Co., Del Monte
has been hosting golfers for nearly a century. The 17th hole (left), a
dogleg-right par 5, is near the glistening Hyatt Regency Hotel.
Another par 5, the 13th (above), demands a tee shot through a
chute of trees.

Golf With a Sense of History
Along the Ocean or Among
The Grandeur of Woodlands.

MONTEREY PENINSULA COUNTRY CLUB

The club's two courses date back to 1926 when R.E. Baldock designed the Shore Course. The Shore and Dunes Courses are meandering and scenic, flanked by pine trees and sand dunes. The picturesque Dunes Course is longer and located farther inland than the Shore, which is short and tight. It was a rotation course for the Crosby for 20 years before Spyglass Hill opened.

The Dunes ninth looks docile but a creek bisects the fairway and flows down the left side.

The Pacific Ocean comes into play at the Monterey Peninsula C.C., as shown in the aerial photograph (left) *and the Dunes 14th* (below)*, where waves crash just below the tee.*

The Golf Course at Quail Lodge (right) is open to guests, while Fort Ord (below) *takes walk-ons on a space-available basis.*

*Two Military Challenges and
A Charming Lodge are a
Credit To the Neighborhood*

THE GOLF CLUB at QUAIL LODGE; AND TWO at FORT ORD

Three other high-quality neighbors of Pebble Beach are the Golf Club at Quail Lodge, formerly known as Carmel Valley Golf and Country Club, and the two courses at Fort Ord, Bayonet and Black Horse. The Golf Club at Quail Lodge is well bunkered. It opens with a long par 5 playing into the prevailing wind. The Bayonet Course at Fort Ord, one of the most difficult on the Monterey Peninsula, serves as a qualifying site for the AT&T Pebble Beach National Pro-Am.

Trees offer a special challenge on the seventh hole at Fort Ord's Bayonet Course, opened in 1954.

Oh Well, There Are Always Those Wonderful Sunsets

The very game itself, once described as an exercise in masochism performed outdoors, is embodied in these shards of an unknown golfer's broken dream of breaking 90, dashed on the rocks of Pebble Beach. Ah, but there is always tomorrow—and with it the hope that one will remember to accelerate through the ball, for heaven's sake.

INDEX

PHOTOGRAPHY AND ILLUSTRATION

Academy of Motion Picture Arts and Sciences, AP/Wide World, The Bancroft Library, Batista Moon Studio, Bill Brooks, Gary Breschini, Rick Browne, Richard A. Bucich, Steve Burton, Colton Hall Museum—City of Monterey, Steve Crouch, Joann Dost/Dost & Evans, Steve Gann, Julian P. Graham, Pat Hathaway Collection, Trudy Haverstat, Ron Hudson, Elena Lagorio, Lawrence Levy, Ray March, Brian Morgan, John Newcomb, Michael O'Hollaren, Bill Paullus, Pebble Beach Company, Photofest/Jagarts, Raven Maps and Images, Tony Roberts, Reynold Ruppel, Smithsonian Institution, Steve Szurlej, Dick Taylor, U.S. Geological Survey's National Earthquake Information Center, Robert Western

IN APPRECIATION:

Jack Davis, Doug Foster, Neal Hotelling, Karen Hunter, Elena and Elmer Lagorio, Cathy Scherzer, Paul Spengler, Diane Stracuzzi